A HANDBOOK (
FOR TEA(

A HANDBOOK OF HINDUISM
FOR TEACHERS

Second Edition

Dermot Killingley (Editor)
Siew-Yue Killingley
Vivien Nowicki
Hari Shukla
David Simmonds

Grevatt & Grevatt
Newcastle upon Tyne

Published by Grevatt & Grevatt, 9 Rectory Drive,
Newcastle upon Tyne NE3 1XT

First published 1980 by Newcastle upon Tyne Education Committee
Second edition, revised and enlarged, 1984
Reprinted 1987

Designed by Grevatt & Grevatt and set by Anne Stals.
Printed in Great Britain by Jasprint, Ltd., 12 Tower Road,
Glover District 11, Washington, Tyne & Wear NE37 2SH.

British Library Cataloguing in Publication Data:

A Handbook of Hinduism for teachers.
  Rev. ed
  1. Hinduism—Study and teaching—Great Britain
  I. Killingley, Dermot
  294.5'07'1041   BL1157.G7

  ISBN 0-9507918-6-5

Price: £7.50 non-net plus carriage charge:
        U.K.: 15% (single-copy orders) or 10% (multiple-copy orders)
        Overseas: 30%. Extra £1.00 bank charges with non-sterling
        payments
        20% trade discount to U.K. booksellers and all U.K.
        educational suppliers (including local education authorities)

All Grevatt & Grevatt publications are non-commercially produced and
priced. This book may be bought direct from the publisher or through
general distributors.

The publisher acknowledges the kind co-operation of the British
Association for the History of Religions in advertising this
publication.

CONTENTS

List of illustrations   viii

Preface   ix

Introduction   1
    0.1. Plan   1
    0.2. Aims   2
    0.3. An introduction to Hinduism   3
    0.4. Spelling and references   5

Part 1: *Hinduism in the Earlier Years*   6
    1.0. Introduction   6
    1.1. Familiarity through play and story   8
        1.1.1. The Blind Men and the Elephant   8
        1.1.2. The Hare in the Moon   9
        1.1.3. King Shibi   9
        1.1.4. An Over-diligent Cat   10
        1.1.5. The Bird with Gold Droppings   10
        1.1.6. The Brahmin and His Goat   11
        1.1.7. The Mice and the Elephants   11
        1.1.8. The Faithful Mongoose   12
        1.1.9. Suggested treatment of an Indian story:
                King Shibi   12
        1.1.10. Activities   13
        1.1.11. Resources   13
    1.2. A feel for Hindu culture: suggested treatment
        of themes   15
    1.3. Factual background: a specimen scheme on Hindu
        festivals   18
        1.3.1. Resources   19

Part 2: *Hinduism in the Later Years*   20
    2.0. Introduction   20
        2.0.1. Resources   22
    2.1. Hindu practices   23
        2.1.0. Introduction   23
        2.1.1. Daily observance   24
        2.1.1.1. Morning, midday and evening worship   26
        2.1.1.2. Worship (pūjā) in the home   26
        2.1.1.3. Resources   27
        2.1.2. Saṃskāras   27
        2.1.2.1. Resources   30
        2.1.3. The temple   30
        2.1.3.1. Small temples   30
        2.1.3.2. Large temples   30
        2.1.3.3. The image   31
        2.1.3.4. Worship (pūjā) in the temple   31
        2.1.3.5. Other functions of the temple   32
        2.1.3.6. Approach   34
        2.1.3.7. Resources   34
        2.1.4. Pilgrimage   34
        2.1.4.1. Resources   36
        2.1.5. Festivals   36

2.1.5.1. Rāma-navamī   37
2.1.5.2. Janmāshtamī   37
2.1.5.3. Navarātri, Durgā Pūjā, Sarasvatī Pūjā
          and Dasarā   38
2.1.5.4. Dīwālī or Dīpāvali   39
2.1.5.5. Shivarātri or Mahāshivarātri   40
2.1.5.6. Holī   40
2.1.5.7. Approach   41
2.1.5.8. Resources   42
2.2. Hindu society   43
  2.2.0. Introduction   43
  2.2.1. Home and family   45
  2.2.2. Caste   47
  2.2.3. Resources   49
2.3. The gods   50
  2.3.0. Introduction   50
  2.3.1. The principal gods of Hinduism   51
  2.3.2. Myths of the gods   55
  2.3.2.1. The Churning of the Ocean   55
  2.3.2.2. The Birth of Ganesha   58
  2.3.2.3. Prahlāda   62
  2.3.2.4. The Descent of the Ganges   63
  2.3.2.5. Krishna   64
  2.3.3. Images of the gods   67
  2.3.4. Learning about the gods   71
  2.3.5. Resources   71
2.4. Hindu ideas   72
  2.4.0. Introduction   72
  2.4.1. Some fundamental Hindu ideas   72
  2.4.1.1. Resources   74
  2.4.2. Some varieties of Hindu doctrine   74
  2.4.2.1. Resources   76
  2.4.3. Hindu ideas in the modern world   76
  2.4.3.1. Resources   77
2.5. Hindu literature   78
  2.5.0. Introduction   78
  2.5.1. The Veda   78
  2.5.2. Post-Vedic Sanskrit literature   79
  2.5.3. Vernacular literature   80
  2.5.4. Secular literature   81
2.6. The historical background of Hinduism   82
  2.6.0. Introduction   82
  2.6.1. Pre-Aryan India   83
  2.6.1.1. Resources   85
  2.6.2. The Aryans and the Veda   86
  2.6.2.1. Resources   88
  2.6.3. Kings and cities   88
  2.6.3.1. Resources   89
  2.6.4. Muslim rule   89
  2.6.4.1. Resources   91
  2.6.5. British rule   91
  2.6.5.1. Resources   93
  2.6.6. Independence   93
  2.6.6.1. Resources   94

2.6.7. Migration   94
  2.6.7.1. Resources   96
2.7. Great people of the Hindu world   97
  2.7.0. Introduction   97
  2.7.1. The Buddha   97
  2.7.2. Ashoka   97
  2.7.3. Shankara   97
  2.7.4. Nānak   98
  2.7.5. Chaitanya   98
  2.7.6. Rānā (King) Pratāp   98
  2.7.7. Mīrā Bāī   98
  2.7.8. Shivājī   99
  2.7.9. Rāmmohun Roy   99
  2.7.10. Lakshmī Bāī   99
  2.7.11. Rāmakrishna   99
  2.7.12. Swāmī Vivekānanda   100
  2.7.13. Rabīndranāth Tagore   101
  2.7.14. Mohandās Karamchand Gāndhī   101
  2.7.15. Sarojinī Naidu   102
  2.7.16. Sarvepalli Rādhākrishnan   103
  2.7.17. Jawaharlāl Nehru   103

Part 3: *Glossary and pronunciation guide*   105
  3.0. Introduction   105
  3.1. The spelling of Indian words   106
  3.2. The spelling used in this book, and how to
       pronounce it   107
  3.3. The layout of the glossary   109
  3.4. Glossary   110

Part 4: *Guide to resources*   124
  4.0. Notes on the bibliography   124
  4.1. Bibliography   125
  4.2. Audio-visual material   134
  4.3. Where to find resources   136

Notes on authors   139

Index   140

LIST OF ILLUSTRATIONS

Forehead marks   25
A small North Indian temple   33
A large South Indian temple   33
A ghāt   35
Brahmā   52
Sarasvatī   53
Vishnu   56
Lakshmī   57
Ganesha   59
Shiva   60
Pārvatī   61
Krishna milking   65
Krishna and Rādhā   66
A linga   69
Nandī   70
Maps: The Indian Subcontinent   84
      Languages of the Subcontinent   85
A Vedic sacrifice   87
Rāmakrishna   100
Vivekānanda   101
Tagore   102
Gāndhī   103
Rādhākrishnan   104

PREFACE

The first edition of this book was published in 1980 by the City of Newcastle upon Tyne Education Committee, with the title *A Handbook of Hinduism: Religious Education Guidelines on Hinduism.* It was primarily intended for distribution to Newcastle schools, to help teachers to carry out the teaching on Hinduism, together with Islam, Judaism and Sikhism, which had been authorized in a Supplement to the Agreed Syllabus. The work attracted considerable attention outside the area, which encouraged us to plan a second edition. It has now been revised throughout and greatly enlarged.

The authors of the original book, who had met frequently to plan the shape of the book and discuss their drafts, met again to prepare this edition. All the material was pooled together to produce a collective work, so that no part is the work of a single author; however, each author has made an individual contribution to the whole. Hari Shukla provided material on Hindu practice and on the situation of Hindus in Britain. Vivien Nowicki and David Simmonds used their classroom experience to devise schemes for introducing Hinduism to young children, as well as preparing material on temples and festivals, and helping to shape the overall plan; Vivien Nowicki also took on the labour of re-writing the guide to resources. Siew-Yue Killingley contributed the stories, myths and pictures, and the guide to pronunciation. The maps were drawn by Mrs. J. Preece of the Audio Visual Centre, University of Newcastle upon Tyne.

Among those who have given us encouragement and advice, I should like to thank Mary Boyce, Carla Contractor, Mary Hayward, Jean Holm, Robert Jackson, Jackie Joicey, Ruth Killingley, Ursula King, Julius Lipner, Gerald Miller, Kenneth Oldfield, Anne Stals and Natalie Waterson.

October 1983   Dermot Killingley
Newcastle upon Tyne

INTRODUCTION

0.1. *PLAN*

The main part of this book has been planned in two sections, headed 'Hinduism in the Earlier Years', mainly for primary schools, and 'Hinduism in the Later Years', mainly for secondary schools.

However, this division should not be interpreted as a rigid division of the syllabus into 5-11 and 11-18 age ranges. For one thing, not all schools are organized according to such a division; and for another, different approaches will suit different classes in the same age-group, or different teachers working with them, so that some of the topics here labelled 'Earlier' will suit some secondary school classes, and vice versa. However, the main principle underlying the division is that in the Earlier section the approach is informal, implicit and pupil-centred, while in the Later section it is more formal, explicit and subject-centred. To enlarge on these differences:

informal/formal: The Earlier section allows more scope for activity and play, and is more suitable for use in an 'integrated day'; the Later section is designed with more formal lessons in mind.

implicit/explicit: The Earlier section attempts to enable pupils to get the feel of Hindu culture, leaving specifically religious ideas and practices to be picked out for attention in the Later section.

pupil-centred/subject-centred: Both sections try to start from what the pupil already knows; but the Earlier section pays more attention to matters within the pupil's experience, while the Later section brings in matters which may be strange to him, but which need to be confronted if he is to reach an adequate understanding of Hinduism.

The aim of this book is to guide rather than to dictate; it is in the nature of Hinduism that there is no minimum requirement which we can expect a teacher, let alone a pupil, to cover. The aim in teaching Hinduism, as explained below (0.2), is to promote respect and under-standing; neither of these will be put across if the teacher is trying to cover a syllabus and ends by dictating a list. Rather, the teacher should feel free to choose the areas in which he can best operate; this involves a consideration of how best he may contribute to the fulfilment of the aims, given the abilities of the pupils and of himself, and the available resources.

0.2. *AIMS*

At all levels, the teaching of Hinduism in schools should contribute to the following interconnected aims:

(a) To promote understanding of the nature of religion, and of religious thought, language and action, taking Hinduism as an example.

(b) To convey a knowledge of what we may expect to find when we encounter Hindu life and thought, and a readiness to understand them.

(c) To encourage respect for Hindu culture among Hindu as well as non-Hindu pupils.

Each of the first two aims has both a cognitive and an affective aspect; the third is chiefly affective, but depends on some cognitive knowledge. The first aim may not, perhaps, be dealt with explicitly until the upper secondary school, but all that has gone before will contribute to it.

0.3. *AN INTRODUCTION TO HINDUISM*

Teachers may be afraid of difficulties in approaching Hinduism, especially if they are used to studying religions which can be defined in credal terms; they may be baffled by what they have learnt about it, or feel that they will never be able to master such a vast subject. For this reason they should feel free to select aspects of Hinduism, and not expect to tell the pupils 'all about' it (0.1). The following outline is intended to help the teacher to find his way, and gives some hints for introducing Hinduism in the classroom.

Hinduism is the religion of the majority of the inhabitants of India. The name 'India' has two meanings:

(a) the political entity which achieved independence as the Dominion of India in 1947 and became the present Republic of India in 1950

(b) the subcontinent of India, which includes Pakistan and Bangladesh. This area has never been a single political unit (though nearly the whole was directly or indirectly under the British Crown from 1858 to 1947), but it has a clear geographical, historical and cultural unity. (The same area, together with Sri Lanka and other neighbouring countries, is also referred to as 'South Asia'.)

In this book, 'India' generally has the second meaning.

'Hindu' is an ancient Persian term for 'Indian'; the Muslims who invaded India from 1,000 A.D. onwards used it to mean the non-Muslim people of India. It was the name of a people and a culture before it was the name of a religion; indeed, it embraced a great variety of peoples and cultures.

Rather than a single creed, founder, organization, canon of scripture or holy place, Hinduism has many which overlap, interact and sometimes conflict. It is hard to define it in terms of belief; perhaps easier in terms of practice. Image-worship, offerings of flowers and fruit, forehead marks, recitation of texts, pilgrimage, reverence for the guru or teacher, the authority of brahmins, rules of purity and pollution regarding food and the body, caste and the sanctity of the cow are highly characteristic of Hinduism; so are belief in rebirth, in the effect of one's actions (karman) in determining one's destiny, in the truth of the Veda, and in a single cause of the manifold universe. Yet many of even these practices and beliefs are rejected by one or another Hindu authority. To study Hinduism we must always be prepared for exceptions and surprises.

Some books (e.g. Zaehner, *Hinduism*; Sen, *Hinduism*) concentrate on the abstract ideas to be found in the learned literature of Hinduism, especially in Sanskrit. Some Sanskrit texts—especially the Upanishads and the *Bhagavadgītā*—are respected and known throughout India, and in modern times have become more widely known through printed translations, popular lectures and broadcasts. They provide a useful point of entry at one level, but they have grave disadvantages. Their ideas are difficult for children to grasp, and their precise meaning is a subject for complex and sometimes acrimonious debate among learned Hindus; and they are outside the experience of most Hindus. Most Hindus receive their religious instruction not from learned texts but from the family and local traditions. They are concerned with the worship of the gods—often local gods, not those of Sanskrit literature—and with the acquisition

of good karman and avoidance of impurity and evil. The approach out-
lined here starts from Hindu practice, bringing in the more abstract
ideas and the learned literature later.

Since one of the aims is to promote respect for Hinduism, special
attention should be given to areas in which disrespect is likely to
arise: e.g. image-worship, food rules, caste, the cow. There is no need
here for apologetics, nor for a neglect of the ways in which Hinduism
itself has protested against some of these matters; rather, the pupil
should understand how they appear to the Hindus themselves. Analogies
may be made with aspects of the pupils' culture which may appear bizarre
to the outsider. On the other hand, an emphasis on sensational or
grotesque features (e.g. Walker, *Hindu World*) should be avoided.

Hindu children should be encouraged to contribute from their first-
hand experience; this may be difficult. Young children in ethnic minorities are often shy of explaining their customs and beliefs to out-
siders; like all children, they are reluctant to let strangers know
about their home life, and they sense a danger, which may be real, that
other children will use the information about what is precious to them
as a new means of ridiculing them. Moreover, because of the variety of
Hinduism, the traditions they have received at home may be different
from what the teacher has learnt. There is a danger that Hindu children
will be left with the impression that either home or school must be
'wrong', or that the knowledge they bring from home is unwanted at
school. With tact and patience, this situation can be an opportunity
for learning about the many-sided nature of Hinduism.

Not only does Hinduism vary in different parts of India, but Hinduism
in traditional villages is different from Hinduism in modern cities, and
Hinduism outside India is different again. Most books on Hindu practice
are based on India; it is worth noting what is retained and what is
abandoned in coming overseas, and this may provide a clue to what Hindus
consider most valuable in Hinduism. Again, to be different is not to
be wrong.

It is equally important to be prepared for variety in language. There
are dozens of languages and hundreds of dialects in India, and the
language of one region is unknown in another. From ancient times,
Sanskrit, the language of religion and also of courtly literature, has
been known all over India, though only to a few; the Muslim dynasties
spread the use of Persian and Urdu, especially in the north; British
rule made English an all-India language, and since independence the use
of Hindi, a widespread language of northern India, has been promoted.
But the diversity remains. Most Indian languages use Sanskrit words
(just as European languages use words derived from Latin and Greek),
especially for religious concepts; but different languages use different
forms of the same Sanskrit word. For instance, Sanskrit *veda* is Hindi
ved, Bengali *bed*, Tamil *vetham* and so on. This leads to difficulties
when these terms are used in English. In English the Sanskrit forms
are generally used, but Hindu pupils may be familiar with other forms.

0.4. *SPELLING AND REFERENCES*

This book uses a popular spelling for Indian words, omitting most of the marks that are used in academic writing to indicate the exact pronunciation; guidance on pronunciation, as well as on the meanings of words, will be found in Part 3. Key terms which it is useful to remember are italicized where they are first explained.

References to other parts of this book are given in the form of section numbers. References to other books, or to articles, are given in a brief form, consisting of the author's surname, title, volume number (if any, in roman figures), and page number, e.g. Thapar and Spear, *A History of India*, II, 106; full author's names, and publication details, will be found in the bibliography (4.1). Ancient texts, however, are referred to by chapter and verse numbers: *Bhagavadgītā*, II, 1 refers to the first verse of the second chapter of the *Bhagavadgītā*.

In the resources lists on particular topics, books and articles are listed first, followed, where appropriate, by audio-visual materials; details of the latter will be found in 4.2.

1.0. *INTRODUCTION*

The aim at this stage is to familiarize children with Hindu culture, and to encourage some respect for it and a tolerant attitude towards cultural differences. The emphasis should be on what the child can relate to, rather than on what is different, exotic or difficult to accept. Such ideas as rebirth, karman, the gods or caste may come up in the course of discussion, but they should not be treated as requirements.

Visits to the school by parents or friends who are familiar with Indian life are particularly useful. They do not have to be Hindus; the fact that Muslims, Sikhs, Jains and Christians share some of the experiences of Hindus is part of the variety of Indian culture. Visitors can talk, show pictures, cook, put on clothes, bring objects which may be familiar to them but not to the children. They may be able to perform music and dance; even if they don't consider themselves musicians, they may be able to sing and drum on a table.

Hindu children should be encouraged to talk about their own experiences, and bring things to school; this will help to make them members of the school community with a contribution of their own, and to respect their own culture. If their experience is different from the teacher's account, this does not mean that either is wrong (see 0.3).

Although the emphasis is on what the non-Hindu child can relate to in Hinduism rather than on what is different, some things are likely to seem strange. Many of the children will have got beyond the stage of remaining unaware of ethnic differences while playing together, and they may seize on the differences they learn about in class to reinforce the sense of strangeness that has arisen from differences of skin colour, dress or diet. The teacher should be sensitive to this possibility, and should be ready to discuss differences openly in order to ensure that learning about Hinduism helps mutual understanding between Hindus and non-Hindus.

For instance, suppose a Hindu girl in the class is already being picked on or avoided by some of the non-Hindu children, and you are telling the story of the Brahmin and the goat (1.1.6). The idea of people not wanting to touch dogs may seem so funny to many of the children that they start teasing the Hindu girl about it. She may have a pet dog at home, for Hindu rules of purity are not so rigid as to make it impossible for a Hindu family in Britain to keep a dog; but that will not protect her from being teased. Now is the time to show that other people's rules are not so strange as one might think, because everybody has rules about what is disgusting to touch, and we should respect other people's as well as our own. You may find some non-Hindus in the class who don't like dogs, as well as perhaps some Hindus who do. Even if you don't, you can ask: 'How would you like it if somebody gave you a slug to cuddle?' Don't worry if the local slug-fancier pipes up; he will soon find himself in the minority, and he knows perfectly well that other people do not share his tastes. In fact, he exemplifies part of the point: different people have different rules, though everyone knows what it feels like to break them. Hindus as well as non-Hindus will have something to learn from this: everyone will learn to expect different people to have different ideas of what is clean and unclean, and to avoid offending them.

The following three stages should be started one after the other, but should overlap:

1. *Familiarity through play and story*: Music, food, pictures, clothes and stories, used to familiarize children with the existence of Indian culture, especially family life.

2. *A feel for Hindu culture*: Exploration of themes familiar from the pupils' experience, showing how they are understood in Hinduism.

3. *Factual background*: India and Indian life; Hindu life in Britain; Hindu festivals; some gods and their mythology; temples and home worship.

1.1. *FAMILIARITY THROUGH PLAY AND STORY*

The aim here is to familiarize children with the existence of Indian culture. Indian culture is mentioned here, rather than specifically Hindu culture, because the different communities in India, and also the Hindu, Sikh and Indian Muslim communities in Britain, have much in common; this common culture can become familiar before the features of particular religious communities are learnt.

Stories can be told to the children, and retold, illustrated, acted or discussed by them. They should be chosen as being attractive to the children and as giving them a feel for the culture, rather than as illustrating particular points of belief or practice, although at the same time they may introduce the children to Hindu life in India, to some Hindu attitudes, and to some of the gods and their mythology.

It is inappropriate to suggest too prescriptive a scheme here, since the nature of this section is informality. The aim is rather to introduce aspects of Indian culture as young children experience their own emotions and relationships in a play situation.

Very young children will readily react to Indian music, food and dress, and these could take their place in the Wendy House or play corner of the reception class, just as Indian stories about animals could coincide with the children's care for classroom pets.

Stories form a major part of the children's collective class activity, and the following, from Indian sources, may be helpful.

1.1.1. *The Blind Men and the Elephant*

Most of us find it very difficult to look at familiar things, places and words in a new light. Children who were born and brought up in Newcastle may be surprised and even irritated if a new child at school, coming from the south of England, invites them home to tea and his mother doesn't produce anything more substantial than a pot of tea and some cakes. What *tea* means partly depends on where we come from, and each meaning is, in a sense, a true meaning of the word. Yet each of us would like to think that our own meaning is the only true one. We hold to our own opinions and often remain blind to other people's ways of looking at things. 'I don't quite see what you're getting at' and 'Why can't you see things from my point of view?' are frequent everyday sentences.

Wise men in India have often argued about the meaning of truth without arriving at an agreed answer. In ancient India, a king who was interested in studying the meaning of truth collected together many stupid men who happened to have been blind from birth, and divided them into groups. He then brought forward an elephant, and allowing each group to feel just one part of the animal, asked them all to describe what an elephant was like.

The first group, after feeling the elephant's head, said that an elephant was like a pot. The second group, however, had felt an ear, and said that an elephant was like a winnowing basket. This is a large, flat basket used for winnowing the harvested whole grain, which is tossed up and down in the basket, the wind blowing the chaff away from the eventually husked grain. But those men who had felt a tusk insisted that an elephant was like the cutting part of a plough. These people were angrily interrupted by those who were convinced that an elephant was like a broom because they were at that very moment firmly clutching the elephant's tail. Finally, the blind men started fighting with each other while the king stood back and laughed, since he could see that each group had got hold of a bit of the truth but nobody was prepared to find out the whole truth.

In real life, of course, we often meet blind people who are more sensitive to the world about them than many sighted people.

1.1.2. *The Hare in the Moon*

English children often hear about the Man in the Moon. Indian children, however, hear about the Hare in the Moon; and what we see as a man's face on the moon, they see as a hare's face. If there is a moon on a clear but breezy night, if you look into a lake, you can see the moon reflected in the rippling surface of the water, as if its face is trembling. Now, this story is about how a wise old hare saved his whole tribe on such a night.

Once upon a time, in India, there was a severe drought. For a long time no rain fell, and every pool dried up. A herd of elephants, nearly dead with thirst, at last discovered a lake of pure water which had somehow remained full. They crashed into it and had a lovely time splashing themselves and each other, and they drank as much as they liked. This they did every day.

However, by the banks of that lake, there lived a tribe of hares, and many of these tiny animals were crushed to death by the big, heavy feet of the clumsy elephants. In time, they would all have been killed. But a wise old hare called Vijaya (which means 'victory')managed to save himself and all the other hares. He pretended to be a messenger from the Hare in the Moon and went to see the leader of the elephants. He told the leader that the Hare in the Moon was very angry that his subjects, the hares, were being killed by the elephants. For the hares, he said, were the guardians of the Moonlake, which belonged to the Hare in the Moon. To prove that this was true, the swift Vijaya led the lumbering elephant to the brink of the lake on a clear moonlit night when there was a breeze ruffling the waters of the lake. He asked the elephant to look in and see the Hare in the Moon trembling with rage. As soon as he did this, the stupid elephant bowed low to the rippling reflection of the moon in the water and promised never to go near the lake of the hares again.

1.1.3. *King Shibi* (see also 1.1.9)

Once there lived a very good and just king called King Shibi. He loved all living things and gave shelter to any creature which needed help. One day, he saw a fierce hawk chasing a frightened and helpless dove. The little dove flew into King Shibi's lap and nestled against him.

Now, the hawk suddenly spoke, and said, 'O King, give me that dove. Since you are so just, you must not let a hawk starve to death by taking away its rightful food.' The king refused to give up the frightened dove, but promised to give the hawk some other meat of the same kind and weight as the dove's. 'Then', said the hawk, 'let me have some of your own flesh.'

The good king was only too pleased to give up his own flesh to save the dove. First he fetched a pair of scales. Unlike our modern scales, scales in olden days were made of a rod with scale-pans hanging on either

side of it. You weighed things by putting metal weights in one pan and
the things to be weighed in the other until the two pans were equally
balanced. Now, using the dove as the metal weight in the one pan, King
Shibi cut off some of his own flesh and put it into the other pan. But
however much of his own flesh he put into that pan, he could not make
the scales balance equally. This was because the dove kept growing
heavier all the time. Finally, as the poor king was nearly dead from
his wounds, he climbed feebly into the scale-pan in a last attempt to
give up his whole self for that gentle dove.

As soon as he had done this, a voice from heaven said, 'Well done,
for you are indeed equal to that very dove that you have been trying to
save.' Suddenly, the fierce hawk changed into Indra, the king of the
gods. The helpless dove changed into Dharma, the gentle spirit of law
and justice. For Indra had planned this trial in order to test King
Shibi's true and just nature and now he knew that King Shibi was as just
as Dharma. And so King Shibi's wounds were healed by the two gods, who
blessed him in many ways before they vanished from view.

1.1.4. *An Over-diligent Cat*

On a high mountain there was a cave in which lived a strong and powerful
lion. Although he was the king of the beasts, he was not able to stop
one of his smallest subjects from annoying him. This was a little mouse.
Every day, when the lion had his afternoon nap, the naughty mouse would
gnaw the tips of the lion's royal mane. The lion found this very annoying indeed, especially because the mouse always darted into his mouse-
hole as soon as the lion woke up fully.

In desperation, the lion coaxed a cat to come and live with him, pam-
pering him with bits of meat from his hunting-trips. The cat was called
Curd Ears, and his creamy ears twitched diligently as he watched the
mouse-hole. So the mouse kept inside his hole and the lion took his
rest undisturbed. Curd Ears grew sleek and fat because whenever the
lion heard the mouse squeaking, he gave Curd Ears more and more to eat
to make him stay as his mouser. The mouse, meanwhile, could not come
out of his hole even to look for food. But one day, the mouse was so
hungry he had to come out of his hole. Curd Ears immediately pounced
on him and swallowed him up.

After this, the lion no longer heard annoying mouse squeaks from the
mouse-hole and so he no longer bothered to feed his retainer. This
story shows that a servant should always make his master need him all
the time. Otherwise, like the over-diligent Curd Ears, he might lose
his job.

1.1.5. *The Bird with Gold Droppings*

Once a hunter found a magic bird which produced gold droppings. He
carefully set a snare and caught the bird, thinking that his fortune
was now made. But when he got the bird home, he became very worried
that the rumour that he owned such a priceless bird would reach the
ears of the king. If that happened, he knew he would be punished for
not giving up the bird to the king. Then, deciding that it was better
to remain poor but safe from the king's envy, he went to the king and
gave him the bird as a gift. The king was very pleased with this present and asked his guards to keep careful watch over the bird.

However, one of the king's advisers said to the king, 'O king, why do

you let this hunter make a fool of you? Who has ever heard of a bird
with gold droppings? Your Majesty should show him what you think of
his incredible story by setting the bird free.' The king thought this
was very wise and he set the bird free. The bird flew upwards, perched
pertly on the lofty archway of the door, and neatly aimed some gold
droppings right in front of the king and his counsellor. Then he
mocked them by reciting in Sanskrit:

> I was the first fool because I was caught;
> The hunter was the next fool, for now he has naught;
> The king the third fool, for he was taught
> By the fourth fool to lose what can't be bought;
> We are a circle of fools as round as a nought.

1.1.6. *The Brahmin and His Goat*

In the Hindu religion, there are many animals that one must not touch,
especially if one is a Brahmin, a member of the highest group of castes.
One of these animals is the dog. This is very hard for English people
to understand because in England, the dog is often a much-loved pet.
So in order to try and understand how disgusting your pet dog can be to
a strict Hindu, you must try and imagine how you would feel if somebody
said to you, 'Do stroke my big, black, beautiful slug. It's all right.
He won't bite. He's so friendly he just wants to climb up your face
and kiss your nose.'

Now, once a stupid Brahmin was carrying home a plump goat on his
shoulder to be sacrificed to the gods. In ancient times Brahmins could
sacrifice animals, but nowadays no Brahmin should kill any living creature. Three clever thieves saw him with his goat and made up a plan to
cheat the simple man. They sat beneath three trees which were all on
the Brahmin's way home.

When the Brahmin reached the first tree, the first thief said, 'O holy
Brahmin, why are you carrying that dog on your shoulder?' 'What?' said
the Brahmin. 'This isn't a dog. It's a goat for sacrifice.'

Then the Brahmin came to the second tree and the second thief said,
'O holy Brahmin, what are you doing with that dog?' The Brahmin put his
goat on the ground, looked at it carefully, put it back on his shoulder,
and went on his way.

Finally, he came to the third tree and the third thief said, 'O holy
Brahmin, how can you carry that dog on your shoulder?' By this time,
the poor Brahmin began to believe that his goat was really a dog. So
he threw it down, ran to a river, and began to purify himself by splashing himself all over with water. In this way, the gullible Brahmin lost
his goat.

This story tells us that we should use our own eyes and minds, and not
believe too easily what other people tell us.

1.1.7. *The Mice and the Elephants*

Those of us who are strong can sometimes hurt those who are weak without meaning to. For instance, a grown-up driving a car carelessly can
easily knock down a small child on his bicycle. And a small child riding
his bicycle, especially on the pavement, can just as easily knock down a
frail old lady. So if we are strong, we must take special care not to
bully weaker people. Instead, we should protect them, for we all depend

on each other. Even the weakest among us can do something for the strongest. Some of you may already know the story of the lion who was helped by a mouse whom he had once protected. In India, there is a similar story about some mice and a herd of elephants.

Once a herd of elephants was looking for water and blindly crashed through a colony of mice, trampling on them and killing thousands of them. The mice went to beg the elephant-king to have mercy on them and to take a different route to the water-hole. After all, they said, one day they might be able to serve the elephant-king in some small way.

Being a just and kind elephant, the elephant-king agreed to lead his herd another way. And so the mice lived on happily. One day, a king was out elephant-hunting and the elephant-king was caught in a snare, together with other elephants from his herd. They were tied securely to many stout trees in the forest and there was no hope of freedom left.

Then the elephant-king suddenly remembered his friends, the mice. By chance, a she-elephant had escaped the hunters and the elephant-king sent her with a message to the mice to ask them to come and help him. The grateful mice came immediately, gnawed through all the ropes which bound the elephants, and set them free.

1.1.8. *The Faithful Mongoose*

Once there was a woman who had a little baby boy. She also had a little mongoose, which she kept as a pet. A mongoose is an animal which is good at killing poisonous snakes. The woman loved the mongoose and brought it up as if it were her own child, but she never trusted it. She was always afraid that one day the mongoose might attack her own little baby.

One day, she took up her earthenware jar and went to fetch some water, telling her husband to keep an eye on the mongoose so that it would not harm the baby. Her husband, however, did not obey her and went out of the house. Soon a black, poisonous snake entered the house and crawled towards the sleeping baby. The mongoose, who loved the baby like a brother, attacked the snake and tore it into many pieces. Then the mongoose ran to greet the woman, who was coming home with her jar of water. He wanted her to praise him for saving the baby. But the mongoose's mouth was all smeared with the blood of the snake which he had just killed, so the woman thought that he must have killed her baby. In her anger and grief, she threw the jar at the mongoose and killed him.

But when she got home and found her baby sleeping safely in his cradle and the bits of dead snake lying about, she mourned for her other son, the faithful mongoose. This story shows us that we should never act rashly or judge others harshly, for we ourselves could be hurt bitterly as a result.

1.1.9. *Suggested Treatment of an Indian Story: King Shibi*

This story can combine teaching about the values of kindness, gentleness and self-sacrifice with an introduction to some Hindu mythology.

Kindness: Children may be invited to talk about being kind and to give examples of this from their own experience, e.g. acts of kindness to parents and friends, looking after animals.

Gentleness: Children should discuss the difference between fighting and forgiving. Which of the two makes the children happier, and why?

Self-sacrifice: Here the children could be given examples of giving up something dear, in order to help others.

The story: This could be read to the children after a short introduction explaining that this Indian story is about a great king, prepared to give up his life for a gentle dove.

Short discussion: Where the moral of the story is stressed. The story may provoke a lively reaction, and children may be encouraged to comment on the characters of Indra and Dharma.

Activities: Mime, dance or a class play, where the children express the values of the story themselves. A frieze for the classroom could be made.

Similar plans can be made for other stories. Not all have equal moral value, but 'The Blind Men and the Elephant' can be used to show the importance of recognizing our own ignorance, and of not laughing at other people's; 'The Hare in the Moon' can show how the strong should not ignore the weak; and so on.

1.1.10. *Activities*

Stories can be acted and illustrated.

Music: use records or cassettes for listening, dance and mime. Live performers may be available; they do not need to be very accomplished.

Food may be eaten and, where appropriate, cooked in class.

Clothes: the children may try on saris, dhotis, etc., or dress dolls.

For all these, the co-operation of Indian children and their parents should be encouraged.

1.1.11. *Resources*

Indian picture-books are available from Books from India, Gohil Emporium, Independent Publishing Co., or Ramakrishna Vedanta Centre (4.3).

Indian publishers of children's books include Children's Book Trust of India, India Book House (which has a children's series, Echo Books), and the Publications Division, Ministry of Information and Broadcasting, Government of India. Some books from the Children's Book Trust of India are listed in Hinnells and Sharpe, *Hinduism*, 207-8 (but note that these books are no longer distributed by Oxfam, as stated there).

Leela, *Fables from the Panchatantra*, and Clark, *Tales from the Panchatantra* are selections of Indian animal stories, retold for young children (for the *Panchatantra* itself, see 2.5.4). Other animal stories are in Khan, *Twenty Jātaka Tales*. *The Tiger, the Brahman and the Jackal* is a story in filmstrip or slide form (4.2).

The *Rāmāyaṇa*, which is the more approachable of the two great Indian epics (2.5.2), is retold in Keskar, *Tales the Ramayana Tells*, Bootha-lingam, *The Children's Ramayana*, and Picard, *The Story of Rama and Sita*. The other epic, the *Mahābhārata*, is retold in Seeger, *The Five Sons of King Pandu*, and Picard, *The Story of the Pandavas*. These stories, originally told in Sanskrit, are familiar in many of the languages of India. They give plenty of material for acting and art work.

Stories of Indian life such as Grant, *A Cow for Jaya*, or Mehta, *Ramu*, can be used to show how Hindus in India live today.

Pictures (travel posters, slides and filmstrips, religious posters, calendars) are useful. The meaning of religious pictures is not important at this stage, but they may provide starting-points for stories. Local Hindu shops, temples or cultural centres may supply them; for other suppliers, see 4.3.

1.2. *A FEEL FOR HINDU CULTURE: SUGGESTED TREATMENT OF THEMES*

The aim here is to develop a feel for Indian, and especially Hindu, culture by showing how it affects relationships with one's surroundings and with people; a further aim is to encourage a respectful and tolerant attitude towards cultural differences.

Themes familiar from the pupils' experience can be explored to show their place in Hinduism. Suggested themes are: Water, Animals, Food, Light, Dancing, Family, Dress. Other themes can, of course, be chosen. The exploration of each theme should be related to what the child is already learning about himself, the world around him and his relationships with others.

The treatment of each theme should start, therefore, with the pupils' experience of it (what do we know about it, what do we need it for, what can we do with it?), and go on to how it is used and thought of by Hindus. Aspects of loving, caring, sharing, helping and forgiving should be stressed.

The following is a suggested outline for the treatment of Water, followed by briefer notes on Animals, Food and Light.

Water

Pose a series of questions, starting with the nature of water and concluding with its special place in Hindu belief and practice.

What? An everyday liquid, changing to ice or steam when cooled or heated. Pupils may already know that it is made up of two elements, hydrogen and oxygen (H_2O).

Where? Found abundantly in nature: sea, rivers, ponds, rain; in other forms, e.g. snow and ice. (At this point it could be shown that water can demonstrate great power: flood, storm, tidal wave.)

Man has controlled water for his own benefit, e.g. dams and reservoirs to store water; canals for transport; water wheels to drive machinery; steam power.

How used? Nature's greatest use is in providing water as a basic requirement for growth, e.g. plants of all types. (This can be demonstrated with seeds.)

Water is used in cooking. Water is used in washing, both of self and belongings, e.g. clothes, cars, etc. This leads on to the idea of cleanliness. We drink water; man cannot survive without it; it is essential to life.

Water is special. Washing and drinking are essential for health. Water is therefore associated with cleanliness and life itself. This leads on to the ideas associated with life itself and cleanliness. Many religions have a special regard for water, e.g. baptism in Christianity; washing before prayer in Islam. In countries where there is often little to be had, water is carefully preserved.

Place of water in Hinduism. From the very beginning, Hindus have had a special regard for water. This is seen in many practices, e.g.:

Water is sipped and the mouth rinsed each morning. Hindus like to bathe each morning, preferably in a river, or else in a temple pool or at home (2.1.1).

In daily pūjā, water is sprinkled on and around the image, which is
always washed and dressed first. Worshippers bring water to the temple
in a copper vessel, with a copper plate and spoon, for the priest to
sprinkle (2.1.1; 2.1.3).

The great rivers of India, particularly the Ganges, are considered
sacred; they are goddesses who have come down from heaven. Pilgrimages
are made to famous bathing places such as Hardwār, Allāhābād and
Vārānasī (Benares) on the Ganges. Ganges water is sipped by the dying
(2.1.4).

Water plays a part in festivals; e.g. at Holī, coloured water is thrown
at people for fun; at some festivals (such as the Kumbha Melā) people
bathe together in rivers in great numbers (2.1.5).

Running water carries away ritual objects when their use is over.
For instance, after the festival of the birth of Krishna a clay model
of his birthplace is carried into a river; a broken image that has been
used in worship is thrown into a river or the sea. Brahmins change
their sacred thread annually and throw the old thread in a river.

All the above could be studied in detail to show how vital a part
water plays in Hinduism.

Similar outlines can be made for other themes; the following notes
may be useful.

Animals

In Hinduism there is a fundamental belief that all living things have
a soul (ātman) which passes from body to body in the cycle of birth and
rebirth. Therefore animals are regarded with great respect, particularly
the following:

Cow: From the very beginning the cow has had an honoured place because
it provides the main necessities of life, such as milk, butter and dung
(which is dried and used for fuel). It is also used for pulling carts
and ploughs.

It is considered sacred and venerated as the embodiment of Mother
Earth. White cows wander at will in cities and countryside; the cow
should never be forced to do anything against its will and should never
be injured. The bull Nandī is the god Shiva's attendant, and his statue
is to be seen in temples of Shiva (2.3.3).

Monkey: Represented by the god Hanuman. It is worshipped because of
the part played by monkeys in the Rāmāyana, the epic of Rāma and Sītā,
where the monkey king, Hanuman, rescued Sītā from captivity on the
island of Sri Lanka. The events are remembered at the festival of
Dasarā (2.1.5).

Elephant: Represented by the elephant-headed god, Ganesha (Shiva's son).
He is thought of as the remover of obstacles, and symbolizes the qualities of patience, strength and wisdom. See also 2.3.2.2.

Snake: Snakes are considered holy, and only killed in an emergency.
Anyone who kills a snake goes into mourning. People put out bowls of
milk to feed snakes.

Food

Generally, Hindus are vegetarians; meat is not eaten because of their
attitude to animal life.

The food generally eaten consists of wheat cakes (chapatti), rice, peas, beans, lentils, other vegetables, milk, curd (yoghurt), ghee (clarified butter) and fruit. The vegetables are often prepared as a curry (see also 2.2.1). Food has an important place in pūjā (2.1.1.2; 2.1.3). It is offered to the god in the temple or at the home shrine. By being offered to the god it is made holy; when people eat it afterwards, they feel they are sharing the god's food. Food which is shared out after offering it to the god is called prasāda. The offerings can be choice fruits, nuts, sweetmeats, etc. They are placed in front of the image, raw food on the left and cooked food on the right.

A lot of the work in Indian villages goes into growing and preparing food. To grow food you have to sow, reap and so on at the right times of year; you have to be conscious of the seasons. Hindu festivals mark particular seasons of the year, and involve offering and eating special kinds of food.

Light

Light and fire can be thought of together. The sun is the source of these, and is worshipped also as the source of life and nourishment. In daily prayers, water is offered to the sun, and sacred mantras, especially the Gāyatrī, an ancient hymn to the sun, are spoken   (see 2.1.1.1).

In pūjā, lights are lit and waved in front of the god (āratī), then placed next to the image. The Festival of Dīwālī celebrates light; houses and gardens are filled with candles and lamps; whole towns and villages are lit up; lights are floated down rivers.

Fire plays an important part in some ceremonies. It is represented by the god Agni; he burns impurities and when sacrifices are offered he carries substances up in the smoke to the gods.

Sacrificial fires are used in the thread-ceremony and in the marriage ceremony. Also, at death, cremation uses the power of fire.

1.3. *FACTUAL BACKGROUND: A SPECIMEN SCHEME ON HINDU FESTIVALS*

The aim here is to offer such factual background information as will help the pupil to develop a cognitive approach to Hindu religion.

In the course of stages 1 and 2, the pupils will have already picked up some of the factual background of Hinduism. In stage 3, more emphasis is placed on the factual background, while still promoting a feel for Hindu culture (stage 2) and providing opportunities for familiarity through play (stage 1). It will still be important to start from what the pupils already know and can experience or relate to.

Some topics suitable for the earlier years are: India and Indian life; Hindu life in Britain; Hindu festivals; some gods and their mythology; temples and temple worship. Details on these topics will be found in Part 2, but the earlier years will require a rather different approach. Here are some suggestions for introducing the topic of festivals in the upper primary school; for fuller information on festivals, see 2.1.5.

Lead lesson: discussion of the meaning of the word 'festival'

The aim of this lesson is to encourage the children to respond to festivals as an important part of life. Much of the lesson will centre upon the children's reactions, and the teacher's building upon these reactions. It is therefore important *not* to introduce any new material here.

What is a festival? E.g. a time of rejoicing, parties, dancing, music or solemn remembrance.

What festivals do we know? E.g. Christmas, April 1, November 5, Id ul Fitr. Not all festivals are religious. Festivals often recall events.

Why do we look forward to festivals and remember them afterwards? E.g. visits, reunions, food, decorations, special clothes.

Lessons on Hindu festivals

After this lead lesson, one or more Hindu festivals may be introduced; it will help if they are dealt with at their proper time of year. Stories connected with the festival should be told (Rāma for Dasarā or Dīwālī in late October or early November; Krishna for Holī in late February or early March); emphasis should be on merrymaking, food, decorations. The pupils' reactions should be discussed.

Other points to bring out are:

Dasarā: Making effigies of Rāvana and burning him, banishing evil with him.

Dīwālī: Victory of light over darkness, shown by lamps. Explore the potential of this symbolism with the children.

Holī: Bonfires, street dancing, throwing red powder and coloured water, practical jokes.

Activities

Stories, poems and pictures by the children, on the festivals and their stories.

Acting of the stories connected with the festivals.

Making effigies of Rāvana; masks of Rāvana and Hanuman; Dīwālī decorations; candle holders; decorated jam-jars; Dīwālī cards.

1.3.1. *Resources*

For resources on particular aspects of Hinduism, see the lists in Part 2. The following are particularly suitable for young children.

Amar Chitra Kathā.
Hinduism (Life Educational Reprints, No. 80).
How a Hindu Prays.
Ramakrishna for Children.

Hinduism (Educational Productions filmstrip).
Hinduism (Concordia filmstrip).
Hinduism (Hugh Baddeley filmstrip).
Holi (filmstrip with tape).

2.0. *INTRODUCTION*

In the later years, from about age 11 onwards, the pupil will be ready
to develop a more explicit awareness of Hinduism as a way of life and
as a religion. This can be considered in terms of the aims stated in
the Introduction (0.2, p. 2).

(a) *Understanding religion*. The Hindu approaches to religious concepts
— the nature of man, the nature of the divine, good and evil, holiness, revelation, worship — should be examined.

(b) *Knowledge of Hinduism*. The pupils should know something of the
practices, literature, beliefs and history of Hinduism; at the same
time, they should be sufficiently familiar with the varied nature
of Hinduism to be open to new knowledge which is different or even
contrary to what they already know.

(c) *Respect*. To overcome hostile attitudes which may develop in the
secondary school, the positive aspects of Hinduism, and its contribution to world culture and the understanding of religion, should
be pointed out.

Children who are already aware of the existence of Hindu culture, and
familiar with some of its stories and practices, will now be ready to
develop their understanding of Hinduism and their knowledge of its ideas,
practices and history. At the same time, if they have been introduced
to more than one religion, they will be beginning to understand what
religion is, how it is expressed in doctrine and ritual, and how it is
related to social organization and history.

The topics covered in sections 2.1 to 2.7 are not intended to form a
syllabus. Each topic provides considerable scope for choice of content
and approach, and it is for the teacher to decide which topics are
appropriate for different groups. The topics, therefore, are not
necessarily to be gone through in the order in which they are presented
here, and they have not been assigned to particular age-groups.

However, the topics which can be expressed in concrete terms will
generally come before the more abstract: Hindu practices and mythology
are easier for younger children to grasp than beliefs about Brahman and
salvation, much of which may be kept for the sixth form. It may also
seem advisable to leave the study of Hindu society, especially caste,
for the upper secondary school; on the other hand, if pupils in the lower
school already have ideas about caste which need to be corrected or put
into perspective, now is the time to do so.

Hindu literature may be studied at any level, if only in the form of
retold stories; the Upanishads and *Bhagavadgītā*, essential for a deep
study of Hindu ideas, can be kept for the sixth form except for selected
passages (2.5). Similarly, some of the 'Great people' can be introduced
early — notably Gāndhī, Rāmakrishna, the Buddha — while others such as
Rādhākrishnan will have little significance except for the sixth-former
(2.7).

The historical background has been deliberately placed low down on the
list, to counterbalance the misleading historicism found in many popular
books and school textbooks on Hinduism. Such books usually start the
study of Hinduism with the Aryan invasion and the Vedas, or, going a

little further back, with the Harappan civilization; but these historical topics have little to do with what Hinduism means to most Hindus,
and are difficult to view clearly—especially for young children beginning their study of Hinduism. The learner may become so stuck in the
remote past, about which a great deal must remain unknown, that he
never looks at present-day Hinduism, and thinks of Hinduism only in the
past tense; or he may gain a false historical perspective, searching for
origins instead of trying to understand things as they are.

Understanding things as they are includes getting to know the Hindus
in this country. Teachers and pupils must be aware that Hinduism is not
just in textbooks, in the past, or in a distant country; it is here and
now, and that is one of the reasons for studying it. Heated classroom
discussions may arise about relations between Hindus and non-Hindus in
this country. Such discussions should not be avoided; they will reveal
to pupils that the study of Hinduism is something that matters to them,
and the ideas that emerge will show the teacher how far the study has
affected pupils' attitudes. A formal debate would be inappropriate,
but a spontaneous outbreak of discussion should be welcomed.

When such a discussion arises, the teacher should assume the status
of chairman, allowing the pupils to argue things out, and moving in
before real fights develop, pointing out how a consideration of some of
the things that have been learnt about Hinduism may help to solve a
problem. We must not forget, too, that a teacher has a pastoral duty
to all pupils, Hindu and non-Hindu alike, and a responsibility for
ensuring that what goes on in school is acceptable to their parents.

For instance, the position of women and restrictions on marriage are
bound to come up for discussion among teenagers. Some pupils will con-
demn Hinduism outright because it does not conform to currently accepted
Western views on these subjects. Others may disagree, and with some
help from the teacher they may be able to formulate two answers to this
kind of attack. Firstly, current Western views are not absolute standards by which all other views should be judged, but only contributions
to a debate in which Hindus as well as others should have a say; and in
stressing duty to society—dharma—Hinduism may have a point. Secondly,
Hindu attitudes may not be as rigid as non-Hindus think. Not all Hindu
women lead restricted lives: look at Mīrā Bāī (2.7.7), Lakshmī Bāī
(2.7.10), or Sarojinī Naidu (2.7.15). Women in Vedic times had more
freedom than in mediaeval times, and they have more freedom now than in
the nineteenth century; so it is possible for Hindu customs and attitudes to change. Hindu women become factory workers, politicians,
doctors, teachers and so on, thus coming into contact with all sorts of
people, without ceasing to be Hindus. All this means that it is not
necessary to follow all the practices described here to be a Hindu.
People remain Hindus if they continue to believe that the life that they
are experiencing between birth and death is only part of a greater whole,
and that we depend for our existence on an infinite being, so long as
they continue to think of that being in a Hindu way.

There may be Hindus in the class who are interested in non-Hindus of
the opposite sex, or non-Hindus who are interested in Hindus. This can
lead to trouble between parents and children which the teacher will not
want to exacerbate. However, without singling out any individuals, it
may be helpful to make the pupils aware of the possibilities open to
them in such a situation, and the likely consequences. They should not
only realize that Hindu parents, like any parents, can be deeply

offended and grieved by behaviour that their children consider right, but should also know what sort of behaviour is likely to offend them. At the same time, they should know that many Hindus, past and present, have protested against some features of Hinduism without ceasing to be Hindus; they have even married non-Hindus without ceasing to be Hindus or breaking away completely from their families.

Some Hindu children may be very anxious to conform to what their elders think right, and to avoid what they regard as the dangers of mixing with non-Hindus. They should be helped to see that at any rate some things non-Hindus do are inoffensive, without feeling obliged to join in everything. Others may be consciously rebellious; they should be helped to see some value in Hinduism without being made to feel that the Hinduism we are talking about belongs to another world in which the tensions they experience have no place.

2.0.1. *Resources*

Jackson (ed.), *Perspectives on World Religions.*
James and Jeffcoate, *The School in the Multi-cultural Society.*
Killingley, 'Hinduism, tolerance and community education.'

2.1. HINDU PRACTICES

2.1.0. Introduction

It is often by noticing differences of practice that children become aware of the existence of different religions: the questions 'Why does he do this, not eat that, wear the other?' invite the answers 'Because he is a Christian, a Jew, a Muslim, a Hindu, a Sikh', and so on. It is in this way, too, that they often become aware of their own inherited religion: 'We do this because we are Christians, or Jews', and so on.

With Hinduism even more than with other religions, it is what people do rather than what they believe that identifies them as Hindus; it is easier to define Hinduism in terms of practice than in terms of belief. Moreover, even when doctrines are discussed in Hinduism, they are closely associated with practice and way of life. It is not enough, for instance, to believe that Brahman is the sole reality; one has to lead a pure life, because it is only when one is purified from selfishness, desire and anger that one is capable of knowing Brahman. The systems that teach belief in God speak not only of knowing God, but of the need to worship and serve him. For Hindus, the teaching of religion involves not only the inculcation of doctrines, but training in a holy way of life in order to bring about an inner transformation.

Although when we teach Hinduism as part of religious education in schools we are not teaching children to be Hindus, we need to be aware of this importance of practice in Hinduism in order to help them to understand Hindus. To a Hindu, religion aims at transforming the animal propensities in a person and enabling him to unfold the divinity that is latent in him. This can only be achieved by living religion consciously every day of one's life, and not reserving it only for some specially holy days. Since Hinduism does not separate religious behaviour from everyday behaviour, the same things are often significant both in a Hindu's relationships with others and in his worship. This is why a feel for Hindu culture (1.2) helps us to understand Hinduism. Food and water, clothing, light and cleansing play a large part in worship. The gestures used in worship (2.1.1) may be used in other contexts also.

A key term in Hinduism is *dharma*. Dharma is everything that a person is obliged to do by his nature as a person; it thus covers religious practice, morality, justice and customary law. Because practice is such an important part of religion to a Hindu, the word dharma is often used in Indian languages to translate the word 'religion'. In ancient times the king was expected to ensure that people in his kingdom behaved according to dharma, and to enforce it through his judges; brahmins compiled textbooks of dharma to guide him (2.5.2).

Today, it is not the business of the modern state to enforce dharma, either in this country or in India; even where the law of the land deals with the same topics as traditional dharma, as in areas such as crime and inheritance, there may be conflict between the two. However, dharma is still followed by Hindus, who learn it from their elders. (For ideas on dharma, see also 1.1.3; 2.4.)

Hinduism holds that there are different dharmas for different people, according to their caste, stage of life, and circumstances, although these different dharmas are all parts of one eternal dharma. The

descriptions given here, therefore, are not laws binding on all Hindus;
they represent what is fairly common and typical, but they cannot
describe all the variety of practices which Hindus learn from their
families. Some practices which have survived for centuries in India
have to be modified in the modern world, both in India and overseas—
food rules, styles of dress, and bathing habits, for instance. If
there are Hindu children in the class, it will be interesting to see
what practices they have learnt and how they differ from what is
described here.

2.1.1. *Daily observance* (see also 2.2.1: Home and family)

All Hindus perform daily prayers because their belief is part of their
life: their religion affects every part of life. Some devout brahmins
spend the whole time, from before sunrise to after sunset, in worship,
purification, religious study, and meditation. Not all Hindus have
time for such elaborate observances, but all follow the principle:
'Whatever you do, whatever you eat...do it as an offering to God'
(*Bhagavadgītā*, IX, 27).
   Daily worship is an individual matter; it may be performed at home,
on a river bank, or in a temple.
   The Brahmins, and others who wear the sacred thread (see 2.1.2),
have five daily obligations:

1. Worship of God, either directly or through the gods. The gods may
   be worshipped by putting a little food in a fire; this form of
   worship is called *homa*, and is taught in the Vedas. A more common
   form of worship is *pūjā*, which will be described below.

2. Reverence to the saints and sages. This may take the form of
   reciting the Veda; a brahmin who does not know any other part of
   the Veda should recite the Gāyatrī Mantra (see below) as a minimum.

3. Honour to parents, elders and ancestors. Offerings of rice and
   water may be made to the ancestors.

4. Giving shelter and alms to the poor, or to holy men. A devout
   family, even though almost starving, will divide whatever food it
   has into two portions; the first goes to the guests and the second
   to the family.

5. Feeding of animals. Hindus believe that all living beings form one
   community.

   For the Hindu every part of life is permeated with religion, and he
or she tends to make into a ritual even the simplest act, such as
working, cleaning oneself or the house, or eating. Here are some of
the things a Hindu may do at the start of the day:

When he gets out of bed, the right foot touches the ground first, to
make a good start to the day. A special prayer may be said as the
foot touches the earth, which was created by God; some say the earth
is a goddess, and it would be very rude to touch her with your foot
without asking permission.

He cleans his teeth and tongue. In an Indian village, he uses a twig
of a special tree, and then throws it away. In towns, disposable
toothbrushes do not grow on trees, but Hindus are still very particular
about keeping clean.

He takes a bath, in a river, a pool or a bathroom. To a Hindu, having
a daily bath has always been an important custom; the ancient cities of
the Harappan civilization, built before 2,000 B.C., had elaborate bath-
rooms and drainage. A Hindu should not have breakfast without saying
his prayers, and he should not say his prayers until he has first bathed
so that he can meet God in a state of cleanliness. Running water is
best for bathing; if he has to use a bathroom, a shower is best because
the water runs from the head, which is the highest and purest part of
the body, down to the feet.

He may mark his forehead with the mark of the god he worships.
Worshippers of Shiva make three horizontal lines with ashes;
worshippers of Vishnu make a mark like a two-pronged fork with white
clay, sometimes with a red prong in the middle.

These preparations are important because of the way the Hindus think
about the human body. For instance, the head is the highest part of
the body, and has to be kept pure; the mouth has to be particularly pure
when sacred words are to be spoken. The feet, being the lowest part,
do not have to be so pure. Touching a person's feet, especially touching them with your head, is a way of showing respect for him, because
it shows that your place is below him. What covers the head has special
meaning for Hindus; so displacing or hitting a Hindu's headgear is a
great insult. It is even worse if you hit his head with your shoe.

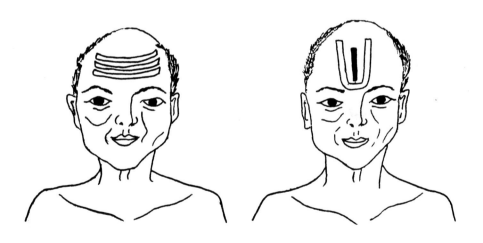

Forehead marks: Vaishnavas make a U-shaped mark
with white clay, with a red mark in the middle;
Shaivas make three white lines with cow-dung ashes.

2.1.1.1. *Morning, midday and evening worship*

Brahmins perform an elaborate worship at morning, noon and evening; if they are busy they omit the noon one. Non-brahmins follow simpler forms.

A brahmin's morning worship begins before sunrise. He faces east; for the evening worship he faces west. The main features of morning worship are:

Sipping water from the hand, for cleanliness.

Tying the hair in a knot.

Breathing exercises, for self-control and concentration. These may be performed in the lotus position: sitting cross-legged with each foot resting on the opposite thigh.

Prayers. These vary according to family tradition, the way one has been taught and individual choice; the best-known are the sacred syllable Om and the Gāyatrī Mantra.

The syllable Om stands for the whole Veda; it can be used as a name of Brahman. It is pronounced at the beginning of many prayers, and is the most solemn of sounds; it is written with a special character: ॐ.

The Gāyatrī Mantra, the Mother of the Vedas, is the best-known of all Vedic verses, being recited over and over by brahmins in daily worship. It is part of a hymn to the sun-god Savitri, and may be translated:

> Let us meditate on the excellent
> splendour of the god Savitri;
> may he stir our thoughts!

The Gāyatrī Mantra may be recited 108 times, counting on a rosary of 108 beads. Other verses from the Vedas may be used, and mantras to one's chosen god.

2.1.1.2. *Worship (pūjā) in the home*

Worship of a god with offerings, mantras or service to an image is called *pūjā*.

Different Hindus offer their main worship to different gods, according to region, family tradition or personal choice; they usually worship other gods as well as the chosen god.

A Hindu house customarily has a room or part of a room set aside for prayer and containing a shrine which may be no more than a shelf on which some flowers are arranged before a little figure or a postcard-sized picture of a god. In India, the shrine is often in the kitchen; this is convenient because purity is important both in the worship of the gods and in the preparation of food. In this country, the shrine may be in a section of a bedroom; in large houses, it may be in a small room by itself.

The god may be worshipped in the form of a picture or image kept in the shrine. Shiva may be worshipped in a linga, and Vishnu in a kind of fossil shell called a shālgrām.

Pūjā is a very bodily form of worship. In the early hours of the day the god is woken with the lighting of a lamp, mantras and music. The image is washed, anointed with ghee, touched with coloured powders, hung with garlands and offered flowers or leaves. Incense is burnt in front of it and āratī—waving of lamps—is performed. Before each

meal, a portion of food is offered to the image; it can then be distributed to the family and guests. Food distributed after being
offered to a god is called *prasāda*, which means 'favour'; for the god
has shown favour to the worshippers by allowing them to eat his left-
over food. In the evening, the image is put to bed.

Gestures and postures, as well as words and offerings, are important
in Hindu worship. Pranāma is kneeling and touching the ground with the
forehead. Namaskāra or anjali is done by placing the hands together,
slightly hollowed, and raising them to the breast or forehead. These
gestures may be made not only to the gods but to people: pranāma may
be done as an act of homage to respected elders such as one's father;
the anjali, with the hands raised to the breast and the head bowed, is
a respectful greeting to anyone. Shaking hands is not a Hindu custom;
when you visit a Hindu home, even if the man of the house shakes hands
with you, it is better to make an anjali to each woman in the family.
When making the anjali, you may say 'namas te', meaning 'homage to you'.

2.1.1.3. *Resources*

How a Hindu Prays.
Parrinder, *A Book of World Religions.*
Sherratt and Hawkin, *Gods and Men.*
Stevenson, *The Rites of the Twice-born*, 209-40.
Yogeshananda, *The Way of the Hindu.*

A Hindu Puja (filmstrip).
Posters, photographs, images (4.3).

2.1.2. *Samskāras*

There are a number of rituals known as samskāras in Hinduism; they
are examples of what is called a rite of passage (or in French *rite de
passage*), initiation, or life-cycle ritual. The study of samskāras
may begin with rites of passage which the pupils already know, or
which exist in cultures known to them. Examples are baptism, confir-
mation, barmitzvah, marriage, ordination, and also the funeral, which
marks a passage from the world of the living to the world of the dead.
Non-religious ceremonies such as civil marriage, graduation, or knight-
ing are also of the nature of rites of passage.

What is common to all these is a change of status (non-member of
church to member; child to adult; living to dead, etc.), i.e. a passage
from one state to another. The rite not only marks the change of status
but also effects it (except in the case of natural changes like adult-
hood or death). Often there is a change of name or title. The person
takes on a new relationship to other people, and sometimes also to the
unseen, spiritual world.

The word samskāra in Sanskrit means 'process, preparation'—a process
by which something is made fit for a particular purpose. In the sense
we are thinking of now, it means a process which prepares a person for
a particular phase of his existence. The word is sometimes translated
'sacrament', since the samskāras of Hinduism are analogous to the sac-
raments of Christianity.

Sanskrit texts speak of a series of samskāras 'from conception to
cremation'. What the texts refer to as the conception ceremony is a
brief rite before intercourse, in which the husband recites mantras

praying for a child to be conceived. Actually the conception ceremony,
if it is performed at all, is only performed before the consummation of
marriage; but there is a series of rites during pregnancy to protect the
unborn child. A person's ritual life, therefore, begins at conception
rather than birth, so that abortion is a great sin. The father rather
than the mother is thought of as the source of life, because he provides
the seed while she is regarded as the field in which the seed is planted.
This view of the importance of the father is related to the patrilineal
structure of the family (2.2.1).

The most important samskaras are the name-giving, the thread-ceremony,
the marriage and the funeral.

Name-giving (nāmadheya) takes place on the eleventh or twelfth day
after birth. The choice of name is very important; it must be
auspicious, and it must not be that of a dead relative, or of the father
or grandfather. The Western custom of naming children after relatives
is, therefore, quite foreign to Hinduism.

It will be interesting to find out the meanings of the names of any
Hindus you know. Often the name is that of a god or hero, goddess or
heroine from mythology. Boys can be called Shiva, Krishna, Rāma or
Arjuna (a hero in the Mahābhārata); girls can be called Lakshmī, Durgā,
Sarasvatī or Sītā (the wife of Rāma). Sometimes the name is an epithet
or description of a god, such as Gopīnātha ('Lord of the cowherd girls',
i.e. Krishna) or Natarājā ('Lord of the dance', i.e. Shiva) for a boy,
or Kumārī ('Princess', i.e. the goddess Durgā) for a girl. Boys' names
may indicate heroism, such as Vijaya 'victory'. Girls' names may indicate beauty, such as Lalitā 'charming', Padminī 'lotus-plant'.

Some names show that the child was granted to the parents by the
favour of a particular god, or has been dedicated by them to a god; the
parents may have prayed and made vows to the god for a long time in the
hope that a child would be born to them. Such names are Devadatta
'given by the god'; Devīprasāda 'favour of the goddess'; Shivadāsa
'servant of Shiva'.

Sometimes all the brothers in a family are given a common element in
their names: for instance, Mahātmā Gāndhī's name was Mohandās, and his
two elder brothers were Lakshmīdās and Krishnadās. Such an element
can run through several generations: for instance, Rabīndranāth
(Ravīndranātha 'Lord of the lord of the sun') Tagore's father was
Devendranātha ('Lord of the lords of gods') and his grandfather was
Dwārakānātha ('Lord of Dwārakā', Krishna's city).

Surnames are in general a development of the nineteenth and twentieth
centuries; during that time many families have found it convenient to
have a surname. Sometimes the surname has developed from one of the
common elements described above: if all the boys' names in a family end
in -*datta* 'given', it is easy for Datta (also spelt Dutt) to become a
surname. Other surnames originated as hereditary titles indicating
occupation or honour; such names are Singh (Sanskrit simha 'lion'),
used by Rājputs and also by Sikhs; Bannerji (Sanskrit vandyopādhyāya
'venerable assistant teacher'), used by Bengali brahmins; Gāndhī 'spice
dealer' and Desāī 'chief, headman', used by Gujaratis and Marathis.
Sometimes English words are used as occupational surnames, such as
Surveyor, Engineer.

The *thread-ceremony* (upanayana) involves putting on the sacred thread,
a loop of string which hangs over the left shoulder and across the
body to the right hip. Brahmin boys may receive the sacred thread 'in

the eighth year after conception' (Manu, II, 37), i.e. at the age of
seven, or later. Kshatriyas and Vaishyas (see 2.2.2) may also receive
it. These three classes are called 'Twice-born' (dvija), because the
thread-ceremony is a second birth which gives a person a new kind of
life; the thread is the badge of a man who is entitled to recite the
Veda and perform Vedic ritual.

The boy who has received the thread begins this new life by studying
the Veda under a teacher (guru, āchārya), who is a second father to
him and must be respected even more than his natural father (Manu, II,
146). Most boys do not in fact learn much of the Veda, but as a
minimum they usually learn to recite the Gāyatrī (see 2.5.1). After
the teaching (whether it lasts a few minutes or twelve years) the pupil
takes leave of the teacher and returns to his family. He is now ready
for marriage.

Marriage is important because it enables a man to have sons who will
carry on his line. The bridegroom comes to the bride's house, where
the ceremony takes place, in a procession; he may ride on a horse or
in a palanquin (a chair carried on poles by a team of men). The essential part of the ceremony is the seven steps in which the bridegroom
leads the bride. The fire, which is the centre of the ancient Vedic
cult, is another important feature of the wedding. Weddings are celebrated very lavishly; the women of both families wear their best
jewellery, the bridegroom is treated like a king or a god, and there
is feasting in both houses for several days.

In a traditional *funeral*, the body is carried to the cremation
ground outside the village, where the pyre is lit by the eldest son
and the ashes are then thrown into a river. In large cities in India,
and among Hindus in this country, cremation does not take place in the
open air but in a modern crematorium. The ashes are collected from
the crematorium and may be sent to a relative in India to be thrown
into an Indian river, preferably into the Ganges at Hardwār; otherwise
they may be thrown into a British river, but it is essential that the
water should be running, not still. No refreshments are served after
a Hindu funeral, as the life-giving process of eating should be kept
separate from anything to do with death; funerals are very inauspicious
occasions, and bad luck can come from them if care is not taken to
conduct them properly. The family and other mourners will go home
and bathe before eating, and they will not eat any sweet food after a
funeral.

According to the Sanskrit law-books, each twice-born man goes through
four stages of life (āshrama): the student of the Veda (brahmachārī),
the householder (grihastha), the hermit (vānaprastha), and the monk
(sannyāsī). The thread-ceremony initiates a boy as a student; the
marriage ceremony initiates him as a householder. A man can become a
hermit by going away to the forest, but only after his sons have had
sons to carry on his line. To be a sannyāsī he has to be initiated by
another sannyāsī; he discards his sacred thread, since thereafter he
takes no part in ritual but concerns himself only with his salvation.
Nowadays the hermit stage is usually omitted, and many men become
sannyāsīs without even passing through the householder stage.

Women have a subordinate ritual status, according to the law-books;
for them, marriage takes the place of the thread-ceremony (Manu, II,
67), and they take part in Vedic rituals only as attendants on their
husbands. A woman can never marry again, even if widowed; but a man

can take a second wife if the first dies, or is infertile, chronically
sick or mad.

On the other hand, women are important in maintaining popular traditions and practices; the women of the family play major roles at a
birth, marriage or death, and at festivals. Among some castes who do
not claim to be twice-born and who do not attempt to follow Vedic
practices, widows are able to remarry.

While the essential features of the samskāras are based on ancient
Sanskrit texts and often go back to Vedic times, many of the details
are popular customs which vary from region to region and from caste to
caste. Samskāras are family occasions, which reinforce the traditions
observed by the family.

2.1.2.1. *Resources*

Pandey, *Hindu Saṃskāras*.
Stevenson, *The Rites of the Twice-born.*

Hinduism (filmstrip, Concordia Films).

2.1.3. *The temple*

A Hindu temple is thought of as a house for the god who is worshipped
in it. A temple may be built for any of the Hindu gods. It is often
built in a place where the god appeared or a miracle occurred, and
pilgrims come to see the god or to pray for a cure or for some form of
success—the birth of a son, for instance, or good exam results.

2.1.3.1. *Small temples*

Many temples are very simple and are found in villages. They are small,
often of wood, with a main room or shrine containing the image. There
may also be a small room for the priest's use, and possibly a veranda
at the entrance. Ordinary worshippers stand in the veranda; only the
priest enters the main room or shrine. At the door are small bells
which the priest rings to warn the god that visitors are approaching.

2.1.3.2. *Large temples*

There are many very large and exceedingly beautiful temples, which
have been built from the seventh century A.D. to the present day. They
are built of stone and are often covered with statues and scenes
portraying the legends associated with the gods. The largest temples
are in South India; notable examples are at Kānchīpuram, Madurai,
Tanjore and Tiruvannāmalai.

The main features of a large temple are the following:

A central shrine containing an image of the god to whom the temple is
dedicated, in which offerings are made. Even in a large temple the
shrine is small and dark, and the walls are uncarved on the inside.
It is at the eastern end of the temple, like the chancel of a church,
and is entered by a doorway on its western side.

Over the shrine is a tall, pointed tower which marks the centre of the
temple; a flag often flies from the top.

In front of the shrine—that is, on the western side—there is a hall,
often a roof supported by pillars, where people congregate, especially

at festival time, and stand facing the shrine.

There may be other shrines to gods who are attendants of the principal god of the temple.

A courtyard surrounds the main building; around the inside of the court-yard there is often a covered way used for processions. The great South Indian temples have a high tower (gopuram) covered with sculpture, over the entrance to the courtyard, and there may be more courtyards sur-rounding it, with more towers.

Since bathing is important in Hindu ritual, there may be a pool of water (a tank, as it is called in India) adjoining the temple or in the courtyard.

The courtyards of very large temples may include halls for dancing, schools and libraries for the study of Sanskrit texts, offices for managing the temple's business, sheds for processional chariots and elephants to pull them, gardens to grow the flowers used in worship, and living quarters for the temple staff.

2.1.3.3. *The image* (See also 2.3.3)

In the temples of most gods, the centre of the shrine is occupied by an image of the god in wood, clay, plaster, stone or bronze. It will have been made by specialist craftsmen according to rules laid down in Sanskrit books, and brought to life by a brahmin in a special ritual (2.3.3).

In temples of Shiva, instead of an image there is a *linga*, which is a round-topped column of stone, on which water, milk or other offerings are poured, or flowers are placed, in worship. The linga, as many Sanskrit texts make clear, is Shiva's phallus; but it is not necessary to mention this in teaching (p. 69). It is sufficient for the children to know that this is the form in which Shiva resides in the temple and receives the offerings.

2.1.3.4. *Worship (pūjā) in the temple*

There is a priest (or priests) at every temple; in a small temple he may be only a part-time priest, and he may be a non-brahmin. Large temples have a full-time staff of brahmins, as well as gardeners, musicians, office staff and so on. The priest's function is to aid the worshipper and to act as an intermediary between the worshipper and the god represented by the image. While women play a large part in home worship, temple worship is normally conducted by men.

Worship consists of offering gifts (food, flowers or clothing) and saying prayers. This takes place at the foot of the image. Food which has been placed in front of the god may be distributed afterwards for the worshippers to eat; it is then called *prasāda* (see 2.1.1).

Worshippers have to take off their shoes—as they would when entering a Hindu home—before they enter the temple. To enter the shrine, they may have to bathe and change their clothes as well; so it is easier to remain in the outer part of the temple. A woman covers her head with the end of her sari when she enters a temple.

It is the priest who makes the offerings and says the prayers; these may be in Sanskrit, which ordinary people would not understand. Priests

have other duties: they wash, dress and decorate the image each day.
  The image may also be worshipped by a priest waving a lamp in front
of it (*āratī*).
  Worshippers are expected to bring offerings to the temple, for the
priest to give to the image. However, the offerings need not be as
costly as the ritual texts seem to require; a piece of thread may be
substituted for a sari, tap water for Ganges water, or a grain of sugar
for an offering of food. The priest will assure the worshippers that
these simple offerings are sufficient if they are made with the right
intention. In the *Bhagavadgītā*, the god Krishna tells his worshippers:

> If anyone gives me with devotion
>   A leaf, a flower, a fruit, or water,
> I accept that gift devotedly given
>   From the giver who gives himself.

                    (*Bhagavadgītā*, IX, 26)

2.1.3.5. *Other functions of the temple*

In the old days the temple was not merely a place of worship, it was
also the centre of all civic and social life. It was often the only
place for public entertainment. The daily routine of rituals performed
in the temple needed the services of priests, florists, musicians,
drummers, dancers, attendants and a host of others. Temples were
wealthy foundations and owned estates to provide income, so they had
accountants to manage their funds.
  Kings and wealthy people erected temples out of generosity or as a
religious duty. To build a temple or to donate gifts for its benefit
were considered acts acquiring merit here and in the hereafter. In the
past, India was known as the land of temples. Even now, India is dotted
with thousands of temples; the largest and most famous are in South
India, where powerful Hindu kingdoms still flourished while North India
was ruled by Muslim dynasties.
  At the larger temples, thousands of devotees come on pilgrimage
(2.1.4) to ask the god for aid, and gratefully give offerings in cash
and kind. The money is used to provide facilities to pilgrims, maintenance, renovation and construction of temples, teaching of the Vedas
and other texts, managing schools and colleges, advancement of art and
culture, and maintenance of hospitals, orphanages and homes for the
poor.
  For Hindu communities outside India, the temple is not only a
religious centre but a social one, and a link with their homeland. It
may sell Hindu images, posters, greetings cards, religious books, and
incense sticks, and provide classes for the study of the *Bhagavadgītā*
and other sacred texts, and for learning Indian languages. People
assemble together for worship in the temple; this often takes place on
Sundays, because of the demands of the working week. For this reason,
a British temple often provides more space for the worshippers than an
Indian temple, where small groups of worshippers may be going in and
out all the time. Conditions in Britain have thus given the temple a
more congregational character than in India. Weddings, which traditionally are home occasions, often take place in the temple, as it provides
a large space for the guests, as well as the right atmosphere. Some
temples in Britain are only rooms in private homes; others are specially

A small North Indian temple, with
the shrine marked by a pointed
tower, a pillared hall, and a porch.

A large South Indian temple, containing
many shrines enclosed in courtyards,
with towered gateways (gopurams).

converted buildings. Hindu temples in Britain are founded and supported
by funds raised among the local Hindu community (2.6.7).

2.1.3.6. *Approach*

It is important to know not only what Hindus do in temples, but what
their attitudes to them are. The god is present in the temple, and
especially in the image or linga (2.3.3). To approach the god one must
be in a holy state, and in Hinduism this means a pure state; that is
why one should bathe and change clothes. To see the god (*darshana*) is
to receive a favour from him, and to go to the temple is an expression
of devotion. The small, dark, plain shrine which contains the infi-
nitely powerful god is like the space within the heart in which the
infinite God dwells.

Pupils should understand and respect the awe and love with which
Hindus approach the temple, and the way in which they hope for favours
from the god who lives in it.

This topic will have greater impact if as much illustrative material
as possible is used. Use large posters (from travel agencies), filmstrips and slides, and pictures from reference books.

A visit to a Hindu temple is obviously desirable, and many British
cities now have one or even more. Directions may be found in *The Asian
Directory* (4.1), or from the National Council of Hindu Temples (4.3),
or from your local Community Relations Officer. Published lists cannot
always be up to date, as temples tend to come and go with the avail-
ability of funds, buildings and staff.

Contact a community representative, such as the secretary of the
temple, and see the temple yourself before bringing a class. It may be
possible to arrange a visit while something specially interesting is
going on—but note that events in the temple may not happen strictly by
the timetable. Pupils should know something about the temple first—
especially that they should take their shoes off before entering, and
remember that people are at worship.

2.1.3.7. *Resources*

Michell, *The Hindu Temple*.
Stevenson, *The Rites of the Twice-born*, 368-417.
Temples of India.
Temples of South India.
Temples of North India.
Kanitkar and Jackson, *Hindus in Britain*.

2.1.4. *Pilgrimage* (see also map, page 84)

There is a craving for religious experience which each Hindu seeks to
satisfy by worship at temples, long pilgrimages and ceremonial bathing.
While religion is an integral part of his life and customs, he feels
the presence of the divine most vividly when he is among great temples
built in stone or carved out of rocks, tiny hill-top and forest shrines,
prayer flags, temple bells, drums and āratī ceremonies. Especially
favoured are places where a god has appeared in visible form or a
miracle has occurred.

Rivers in India are considered sacred by the Hindus. Of the many
rivers, the Ganges, Jumna, Narmadā, Godāvarī, Krishnā and Kāverī are

A ghāt: a place on a river bank for bathing and drawing water.

particularly sacred. The Hindus believe that a bath in their waters
washes away all sins (cf. 2.3.2.4). There are also sacred mountains,
such as Kailāsa in the Himālayas, which is Shiva's home, Mount Ābū in
Rājasthān, and Tirumalai, near Tirupati in South India, sacred to
Vishnu.

Many places of pilgrimage are on rivers. On the Ganges, the most
sacred of all, are Rishikesh and Hardwār, where the river descends from
the Himālayas; Allāhābād or Prayāga, at its confluence with the Jumnā;
and Vārānasī or Benares, the most sacred of all Hindu cities. On the
Jumnā are places associated with Krishna (2.3.2.5): Mathurā, where he
was born; Gokula and Vrindāvan, where he lived among the cowherds; and
Kurukshetra, where he taught Arjuna. (Kurukshetra was already famous
in Vedic times, for the performance of sacrifices.) Dwārakā, on the
coast of Gujarāt in Western India, is the place where Krishna died.

On the east coast, Purī is famous for its temple of Vishnu, where he
has the title Jagannātha, 'Lord of the world' (his great temple chariot
there has given us the word 'juggernaut'). In South India, Tirupati,
Chidambaram, Srīrangam, Madurai and Rāmeswaram are marked by magnificent
towered temples (2.1.3.2). Rāmeswaram, on an island between the Indian
mainland and Sri Lanka, marks Rāma's route on his expedition against
Rāvana.

Hindu places of pilgrimage are not confined to India. In Malaysia,
East Africa and even England there are places sanctified by miracles
or by the lives of holy men.

It is the wish of every Hindu to go on a pilgrimage at least once in

their lifetime. There is no fixed time to go on a pilgrimage but most
Hindus make their pilgrimages coincide with important festivals such as
the Kumbha Melā, which is a bathing festival and the oldest fair in
India.

The Kumbha Melā festival is held at Allāhābād, where the sacred rivers
Ganges and Jumna meet, in the month of Māgh (January-February). Thousands of pilgrims, young and old, rich and poor, holy men and house-
holders pour into the Melā (assembly) area, and settle into tents and
makeshift huts. The pilgrims are rowed in thousands of boats to the
sacred confluence, to immerse themselves in the water at the most auspicious hour of the day. This bathing festival is said to attract the
largest crowd in the world.

At all holy places on the rivers, there are a number of bathing
ghats; the word ghat means a landing place or a flight of stone steps
leading down to a river. At Vārānasī on the Ganges, there are more than
seventy bathing ghāts extending along about six kilometres of the river
bank. Each ghāt at Vārānasī has its own historical and religious
importance. The Tulsī Ghāt, for example, is named after the saint-poet
Tulsīdās. It is believed that it was there that he wrote the famous
epic poem *Rām Charit Mānas*, a Hindi version of the *Rāmāyama*, over four
hundred years ago.

Hindus go on pilgrimages in order to have a closer experience of their
chosen god, to wash away sins with a bath in a holy river, to pray for
favours from the god or to give thanks for favours granted. Someone
who longs for the birth of a child, or for a child to be cured of long
sickness, may go on pilgrimage to a place where a god is believed to
have appeared or granted miracles in the past, to pray. Or he may pray
first, and make a vow that if his prayers are granted he will go on
pilgrimage, and make an offering of money, produce or cloth to a famous
temple. Many pilgrims go by train or bus; others walk; others, to show
their extreme devotion, make their journey even more difficult by
measuring their length on the ground all along the way. But many pilgrims enjoy their visit: they meet old friends, see the sights, wear
fine clothes, and eat festive food. Places of pilgrimage are full of
fun, with shops selling local handicrafts (Vārānasī is famous for brass-
ware as well as holiness), eating shops and street showmen.

2.1.4.1. *Resources*

Thomas, *Festivals and Holidays of India.*
Klostermaier, *Hindu and Christian in Vrindaban.*

2.1.5. *Festivals*

Festivals, feasts and rituals are the best teachers of all. Every
festival symbolizes the code of life, so DASERA, DIWALI and HOLI are
all celebrations of the victory of right over wrong. During this
time epics are enacted which leave a deep impression on the tender
mind.   (V. Khadke in Cole, *Religion in the Multi-faith School*)

Festivals are an important part of the way in which Hindu children
assimilate Hinduism, and by examining them pupils can gain an insight
into Hindu experience.

Hinduism does not make a sharp division between work, play, and
worship; a festival may involve all three, and can be looked at in

many ways and at different levels.

The Hindu year is punctuated by festivals; the exact list differs from region to region. The Hindu calendar is based on the phases of the moon, so that the date of a festival according to our calendar varies from year to year; but it always falls in the same season. The exact dates for some festivals, including those described here, may be found each year in the *Calendar of Religious Festivals* published by the Shap Working Party (4.3). There are various ways of reckoning the beginning of the year: it may be between mid-March and mid-April, or around June or October, in each case beginning with the new moon; the Tamils, however, start their year not by the moon but by the sun, at the spring equinox. You may get several answers, therefore, to the question 'When is the Hindu New Year?'. The festivals described below are the best-known throughout India, though different groups of Hindus give prominence to different ones, and to different aspects of them.

2.1.5.1. *Rāma-navamī* (late March or April)

Rāma's birthday is celebrated on this day, the ninth day of the waxing moon; the name means 'Rāma's ninth'. Sometimes the festival begins on the first day of the lunar month and goes on for nine days. Pūjā to Rāma takes place in the home shrines, but many people attend the temple where worship is offered to Rāma, and where priests read aloud the events in Rāma's life from the *Rāmāyana*. Worship also involves the singing of the Rāma-nāma—the hundred and eight names of Rāma. Whenever Rāma is worshipped Hanuman must be present to hear it; therefore a seat is always set aside for the monkey king. The celebrations also include processions in which an image of Rāma is carried round the neighbourhood.

As it is a fast day, certain foods are not eaten; for instance, cereals, salt and ordinary vegetables. However, on this day families do enjoy eating some of the more unusual delicacies which they cannot normally afford.

2.1.5.2. *Janmāshtamī* (July or early August)

This day, 'the eighth of the birth' (so called because it is the eighth day of the waning moon), is the birthday of the playful but protective god Krishna (2.3.2.5). Krishna's birth took place on a dark stormy night in prison. Many Hindus go to the temple to await the hour of his birth at midnight, and greet it with singing and dancing or with cries of 'Victory!'. Everyone shares sweet foods just like those given to an Indian mother shortly after her baby is born. Sometimes the priests throw curds into the air on to the worshippers. Stories of Krishna's life, especially those in the *Bhāgavata Purāna*, are recited, and dances and dramas based on them are performed. The third part of E. M. Forster's *A Passage to India* opens with a suitably playful and affectionate description of a Janmāshtami festival.

This festival is naturally most important for those who worship Krishna as their favourite god, while Rāma-navamī is more important for devotees of Rāma. The contrasting characters of these two avatāras of Vishnu are reflected in the relatively solemn rejoicing at the birth of Rāma and the more uninhibited festivities for Krishna.

2.1.5.3. *Navarātri, Durgā Pūjā, Sarasvatī Pūjā and Dasarā*
(late September or early October)

This is a sequence of ten days of varying significance for different Hindus.

Navarātri means 'nine nights', and the main celebrations take place after sunset; some people fast until after the evening pūjā. The worship is offered to the goddess Durgā, or else to three goddesses: Durgā the wife of Shiva, Lakshmī the wife of Vishnu, and Sarasvatī the wife of Brahmā. These three are either worshipped together or for three nights each. Women are prominent in Navarātri, and little girls may be dressed up to represent Durgā.

Durgā's great exploit is the killing of a buffalo-demon whom none of the gods could defeat. She fought him for nine days, and killed him on the tenth. The tenth day, Dasarā, is therefore a day of victory; some people call it Vijaya Dashamī, 'victorious tenth'.

The whole ten-day period is the most popular and spectacular festival of Bengal, where it is called Durgā Pūjā. It is a time, particularly, for newly-married daughters to leave their husbands' houses to pay visits to their parents at their family home. The *Chandī-Māhātmya*, a poem telling the story of the victory of Durgā over the forces of evil, is recited. On the tenth day, the statue of Durgā made for the period of the celebrations, and used as a focus of worship during the ten days, is taken in a joyful procession to a river bank and put into the water. As it sinks the people rejoice, believing that all unhappiness and ill-fortune have been carried away. In Calcutta especially, the streets are illuminated with elaborate displays of electric lighting.

This period is also associated with Rāma, because before setting out to defeat the demon Rāvana, he fasted and prayed to Durgā at this time of the year. On the tenth day, Dasarā, he set out on his expedition against Rāvana; the defeat of Rāvana is therefore celebrated on this day, although it did not happen until the following spring. Bonfires are lit; fireworks and sparklers are set off. Huge effigies of Rāvana are burned amidst general rejoicing. In Delhi, huge celebrations are held at which an effigy of Rāvana over thirty metres high is burned and there is a gigantic display of fireworks.

Besides this, Navarātri is a time of social gatherings and family reunions; families conduct pūjā to Rāma and Sītā. Rāma represents security and protection from evil; Sītā, constancy and faithfulness. People are reminded that good is more powerful than evil, though it requires a struggle to defend it, and that they should be loyal and friendly to each other.

Dasarā is also the day on which the five Pāndava brothers, the heroes of the *Mahābhārata*, took up arms again after thirteen years, and set out to make war on their usurping cousins. Its association with Rāma and the Pāndavas means that Dasarā belongs especially to kings and warriors; it marks the beginning of the campaigning season, when Hindu kings held military parades and inspected their armouries. Even Muslim rulers got Hindu deputies to hold Dasarā ceremonies, and the East India Company's army used to have its flags and weapons blessed by brahmins.

In South and West India, Sarasvatī Pūjā takes place on the seventh, eighth and ninth days of Navarātri. Sarasvatī is the goddess of learning and the arts, and this is a time when people remember the importance of study. School books, and books of Hindu scriptures, are collected together and worshipped in each house, and some children begin to learn their letters at this time.

Navarātri and Dasarā come at the time of year when calm autumn weather begins, after the violent monsoon rains and swollen rivers; nature is tamed, and flooded roads become passable again. The taming of nature is reflected in the myths of victory over demons; the clearing of the roads makes possible military expeditions, which are symbolized by the expeditions of Rāma and the Pāndavas, and also family reunions, symbolized by Rāma's reunion with Sītā.

2.1.5.4. *Dīwālī or Dīpāvali* (late October or early November)

This festival lasts for up to five days, around the time of the new moon following Navarātri. The name means 'a row of lamps', and the festival can be recognized by the rows of little oil lamps around each Hindu house at night.

At this time the people remember various stories about the gods. One of the most popular is taken from the *Rāmāyana*; it relates Rāma and Sītā's triumphal return to their kingdom, Ayodhyā, and Rāma's coronation. In Vārānasī the entire story narrated in the *Rāmāyana* is told over a thirty-day period; it ends with a short pageant of Rāma's victory procession. Another story concerns the goddess Lakshmī, the consort of Vishnu, who visits houses lit by many lamps bringing gifts and promising prosperity throughout the coming year to all those in the household.

Vishnu's defeat of the demon Bali is another reason for celebrating Dīwālī. According to the story, Bali gained control of the world; he then decided to perform a great sacrifice so he could become the master of the heavens and the gods as well. Vishnu thought up a plan to defeat Bali. He took the form of a dwarf and went to beg for alms from Bali. Bali responded by offering Vishnu as much land as he could cover in three strides; thereupon Vishnu grew so large that he covered the earth and heaven in two strides. With the third stride he stepped on Bali's head and pushed him down to the underworld, where he still rules. However, by touching Vishnu's foot with his head, Bali became a worshipper of Vishnu (as did Kālīya, 2.3.2.5); Vishnu was merciful to him, and allowed him to return to earth for one day in the year, namely Dīwālī.

Dīwālī is a celebration of the victory of light over darkness. Homes, temples, streets and shops are brightly decorated and illuminated. Rows of little oil lamps light up the garden paths of the houses, and children carry lamps. More lamps are put round the outside of public buildings, so that the darkness of the night is lit up with thousands of flames; in Bengal, girls place floating lamps on the rivers. Some say that the lamps light a path for the dead, leading them to heaven.

Dīwālī is also a time of renewal; in North India it is the beginning of the new year. Houses are swept clean, brass ornaments are polished, and working animals are washed, groomed and decorated. People wear new clothes, and begin using new utensils and tools. Debts are paid before Dīwālī, and businessmen clean out their shops and offices, and open new account books, worshipping them together with Lakshmī, the goddess of wealth. Children are lectured and told to follow the example of their elders and turn over a new leaf. Some people stay awake all night to see the new year in.

Merry-making is also associated with the new year. Presents are given, greetings cards are sent, friends and relatives are visited, and there

are special foods and sweets. British Hindus, when talking to other
British people, often refer to Dīwālī as 'our Christmas'.
    Pūjā to Rāma, Sītā and Lakshmī takes place in the home. Bhajans
(devotional songs) are sung, and devotional dances performed. Āratī
(the ceremony of waving lights before the image) takes place in temples.

2.1.5.5. *Shivarātri or Mahāshivarātri* (February or early March)

The name of this festival means 'night sacred to Shiva'; this is because
worship goes on throughout the night. Compared to other festivals it is
a solemn occasion marked by fasting. Some devotees of Shiva do not sleep,
eat or drink for thirty-six hours.
    During the night, Shiva is worshipped in shrines containing his symbol,
the linga (2.3.3), around which people assemble and perform pūjā. Offerings are made by pouring milk, curds, ghee, and honey over the linga;
the leaves of the bilva, a tree sacred to Shiva, are also scattered over
it. When the fast ends in the morning, much feasting follows, with sweet
potatoes and cucumbers among the many foods eaten. It is also believed
that unmarried girls should keep vigil throughout the night so that Shiva
can help them to find a suitable husband.
    At the festival the people remember a story which helps to explain why
they fast and keep a watch throughout the night. The story is that once,
on this night of the year, a hunter who had caught nothing all day climbed
a tree to shelter from the beasts of prey. He had nothing to eat, and
could not sleep because of the cold. He passed the time plucking leaves
off the tree; or perhaps his shivering shook them off, or he plucked them
to give himself a view of the ground in case a deer came. It happened
that the tree was a bilva tree, and at its foot was a linga. There are
many versions of the story, but the point of them all is that by staying
awake and fasting, and scattering bilva leaves over the linga, he was
accidentally worshipping Shiva. His sins were removed (and hunters are
very sinful people, because they kill animals), and Shiva blessed him.
    For the members of the Ārya Samāj (2.4.3), the reform movement founded
in 1875, this night has a new significance. Their founder, Dayānanda
Sarasvatī, was required as a boy to join the Shivarātri vigil, but soon
found that the other worshippers were all asleep, and that mice were
running over the linga to eat the offerings. The boy decided that a god
who allowed such disrespect was not worth worshipping, and spent the
rest of his life searching for the true Hinduism, in which, he believed,
God must be worshipped without the use of images or other objects. The
Ārya Samāj therefore commemorates its founder's enlightenment on this
night.

2.1.5.6. *Holī* (February or March)

This festival is held on the day of the full moon at the end of the cool
season and the beginning of spring. The origin of the name Holī is
obscure; it has nothing to do with the English word 'holy'.
    In India, spring is the season of love, so Holī is sacred to Kāma, the
god of love, and to the great lover, Krishna (2.3.2.5). It celebrates
the games Krishna played with the cowherd girls, and the beginning of
his love for Rādhā, one of the cowherd girls. According to the legend,
Krishna was brought up by foster-parents as a cowherd; he was a mis-
chievous boy, and often bewildered his foster-mother with his tricks.

Appropriately, then, Holī is a time for playing practical jokes.

At home there is pūjā to Krishna, and in the temples stories about Krishna and Rādhā are recited and acted. However, much of the time during the festival is spent outside; in the streets and squares, bonfires are lit and dances performed. Processions are held in which bullocks pull decorated carts on which are images of Krishna and Rādhā on swings which are adorned with flowers.

Holī is a time for fun. Boys go about the streets spraying people with coloured water from squirts, or throwing coloured powder at them. It is not safe to go out in good clothes, and if people return home coloured from head to foot it is a sign they have really enjoyed themselves. Krishna and the cowherd girls are said to have sprayed each other in this way at Holī, so that those who do so now are imitating them and joining in the divine fun.

The rules of everyday life are relaxed at Holī: respectable people can be treated disrespectfully or even insulted, and some high-caste people consider it good luck to touch a low-caste person on this day—though they take care to have a bath afterwards.

In Western India, a bonfire is an important part of Holī. The boys go round the houses for days beforehand, collecting wood and cow-dung—a regular household fuel in India—to build their neighbourhood bonfire. When the fire is lit on Holī day, people walk round it shouting abuse at it, and throwing in dates and other food.

The explanation they give for this is that the fire represents a witch called Holikā. Some say that Holikā terrorized the country and ate children, until the people rose up and burnt her. As they did so, they yelled so that the other witches and demons would not hear her cries. But to avoid trouble from her afterwards, they also propitiated her with offerings of dates. If it seems strange to think of Holikā both as an enemy to be destroyed and insulted, and as a friend to be fed with offerings, it may help to remember how English children collect pennies 'for the guy' before they burn him.

Another version of the Holikā story connects her with Prahlāda, the mythical devotee of Vishnu (2.3.2.3). In this version, Prahlāda's father, the demon Hiranyakashipu, also had a daughter or a sister, the witch Holikā. When Hiranyakashipu was angered by Prahlāda's devotion to Vishnu, he got Holikā to take Prahlāda on her lap, hoping that her witchcraft would enable her to burn Prahlāda and remain unharmed herself. But, as with all his other attempts to destroy Prahlāda, Hiranyakashipu's plot failed and Holikā was burnt instead.

2.1.5.7. *Approach*

For young pupils, we should naturally emphasize the 'fun' side of festivals, and the part they play in the experience of children. The pupils' own experience of Christmas, Easter or non-religious dates like January 1, April 1 or November 5 may be taken as a starting-point for their understanding of what a festival is. For an approach to festivals for young children, see 1.3.

For more advanced pupils, there are other directions in which festivals may be explored:

(a) The beliefs expressed and reinforced by festivals. Rāma's victory over Rāvana, and his role as protector against oppression, are

related and enacted at Rāma-navamī and Dasarā. Vishnu's preservation
of the world is remembered at Dīwālī. Shiva's power to remove the
sins of his worshippers is remembered at Shivarātri.

(b) The myths and legends used in explaining the festivals. More than
one story may be told to explain the same set of actions, as in the
stories of Rāma and of the Pāndavas at Dasarā, and the different
stories explaining Holī.

(c) The social role of festivals. Dasarā provided the rājās of mediaeval and British times with an opportunity to parade their armies;
Dīwālī sets a time for the discharge of debts; Holī provides a social
safety-valve by relaxing the rules which are rigidly held for the
rest of the year (compare April 1st, office Christmas parties, etc.).

(d) Festivals as an expression of the yearly cycle of nature and of man's
work. The Holī bonfire marks the destruction of winter; Dasarā is
a day of victory over the dangers of the rainy season. Dīwālī starts
a new financial year, and marks the beginning of the year's round of
work.

2.1.5.8. *Resources*

This topic calls for colourful treatment; use any pictures, figures,
decorations, etc. that can be bought from Indian shops or borrowed from
Hindu homes.

Printed Dīwālī greetings cards may be on sale during October in this
country, at Indian shops or at Hindu temples.

Calendar of Religious Festivals.
Divali and Other Aspects of Hinduism.
Hannaford, *Holi.*
Kanitkar and Jackson, *Hindus in Britain.*
Marsh, *Divali.*
Mehta, *Ramu.*
Nowicki, 'Hindu festivals.'
Stevenson, *The Rites of the Twice-born.*
Thomas, *Festivals and Holidays of India.*

BBC audio-cassettes, *Festivals—Hindu; Navaratri.*
Hindu Festivals (4 wallcharts).
Holi (filmstrip with tape).
Who is My Neighbour? (12 slides on Holi).

2.2. HINDU SOCIETY

2.2.0. Introduction

The practices described in section 2.1 take place within the context of Hindu society; they are perpetuated by Hindu society and at the same time they reinforce the structure of that society.

Hindu society is a vast subject and a fruitful field for anthropologists and sociologists. These scholars—Indian, European and American—study in great detail the patterns of kinship and inheritance, village and caste organization, the way traditions are handed on, the roles of the elders, priests and teachers, and so on. Systematic studies of this kind are mainly a product of the present century; but behind them lie the contributions of nineteenth-century missionaries, administrators and reformers who found themselves needing to understand the society in which they worked.

We can only deal with a small part of the subject of Hindu society in a school's syllabus, but we can bear in mind some points that have emerged from the modern study of Hindu society. Firstly, the more one tries to say about it, the more one has to confine oneself to a particular community in a particular area: all generalizations are dangerous. Secondly, despite this variety, certain features like the joint family and caste are typical of Hindu society. Thirdly, these features survive modern pressures, just as they have survived changes in the past; they are adapted rather than abandoned.

Though Hinduism is a highly individualistic religion, in that it allows people to have their own ideas about the nature of divine reality and to pursue their own way towards perfection, the continuity of Hinduism is maintained by Hindu society. Most Hindus are born and brought up as Hindus; the series of saṃskāras which integrates them into the Hindu community begins even before their birth (see 2.1.2). Conversion to Hinduism is a modern idea, and by no means generally accepted; for though some Westerners take up yoga, Transcendental Meditation, or various forms of Hindu belief or practice, it is debatable whether they have become Hindus, and most Hindus would not regard them as members of Hindu society.

The two aspects of Hindu society which will be discussed here are the family and caste. These aspects are the ones which people in this country are most likely to have heard of, and what they have heard may not be favourable. Restrictions on women and girls, child marriage, arranged marriage, caste privilege and untouchability: these are all matters which the teacher will have to handle delicately and sensitively. If we spoke of them as some Victorian missionaries and imperialists did, as examples of what Hindus need to be rescued from, we would turn the lesson into a polemic against Hinduism. If we ignored them, we would leave the pupils to perpetuate the old attitudes, and if we claimed that such things no longer exist, they would (with some reason) not believe us. If we said that these practices were right for Hindus but not for others, we would be saying in effect that Hindus are a different kind of people, and thus perpetuating racial prejudice and double standards. If, on the other hand, we defended them uncritically, on apparently scientific lines, we would not only be unlikely to convince non-Hindus, but we would offend many Hindus. For Hindus are not uncritical

of their inherited institutions; they do not perpetuate them unchanged,
but adapt them to new circumstances and new climates of thought.

The nineteenth-century Hindu preacher Vivekānanda made some pertinent
remarks about Westerners who came to India and praised everything they
found there. Addressing a Hindu audience, he stressed the difference
between himself and such uncritical admirers of Hindu society:

> I have not been imported from some foreign land to come and save you,
> that I should countenance all your foolish customs and give scientific
> explanations for them; it does not cost our foreign friends anything,
> they can well afford to do so. You cheer them up and heap applause
> upon them, and that is the acme of their ambition.
>
> (Vivekānanda, *Complete Works*, V, 457)

Vivekānanda was referring to Western visitors to India in the 1890s,
especially members of the Theosophical Society; but the kind of people
he was talking about still exists. While such foreign admirers may bring
fresh insights to some aspects of Hinduism, they may not have a real
understanding of everything that they admire; they may merely be discontented with Western society, and using Hinduism as a refuge from it.

To understand Hindu society, we have to be aware of the tensions within
it. At the same time, we must be aware of its positive value, and avoid
giving the impression that because people who are not used to it would
be discontented if they were transplanted into it, everyone in it must
be discontented too. The Hindu family, like any other type of family,
supports its members as well as restricting them, and is better at providing for the old than the modern nuclear family; caste also has a
supportive function, providing security and preparing different people
for different places in society. Arranged marriage, too, works well
and fairly happily so long as the roles of wife and husband are more or
less stereotyped, so long as young couples are likely to follow the same
way of life as their parents and grandparents have experienced, and so
long as families are well known to one another. To know that your
parents have chosen or will choose for you, provides security if dating,
courting and going steady are not part of your culture. Child marriage,
though it has its dark sides and has gone out of favour since the nineteenth century, can be a prudent way of ensuring this security: after
the wedding the bride remains at her parents' house until her boy husband is old enough to bring her home as his wife.

Discontent with Hindu society and struggles between individual and
family are nothing new: we find them in the lives of saints such as
Chaitanya, Mīrā Bāī and Rāmakrishna (see 2.7). Intense devotion to God
(bhakti) and rejection of everything to do with the world (sannyāsa)
bring such people into conflict with their families who are trying to
provide them with a comfortable future and prepare them to carry on the
family traditions; they lead them to reject the rules and privileges of
their caste. Discontent and tension come also with social change: when
modern education or employment bring young people together in circumstances that allow them to choose their own partners and life styles,
they are likely to rebel against the choices made for them by their
elders, and when educational qualifications and business enterprise have
more economic value than inherited property and skills learnt in the
family, duty to family elders becomes burdensome. Hindus in the modern
world are well aware of the tensions between the individual and society.

But the claims of society are still strong. In common with other Asians, many Hindus working in Britain maintain close links with families in India and support them with remittances; Hindus generally respect their elders and feel bound by ties of kinship even to distant cousins. In contrast to the restless individualism of the modern Western world, they know that the individual's life can only have meaning as a part of the life of society—unless he is a saint.

2.2.1. *Home and family*

The basis of Indian life is the family, which forms a large but very solid unit. The typical Hindu family is the patrilineal joint family: that is, kinship through the male line is more important than kinship through the female line, and the brothers, sons, grandsons and great-grandsons of the head of the house, with any of their sisters who are not married, form one family. They may not actually live in the same place or hand over all their earnings to the head of the family, but they still feel that they belong to the ancestral home, and consider that their elders have a claim on their wealth. A Hindu who has gone to work in a city, in India or overseas, often regards his city house or flat only as a lodging, and goes back whenever he can to his real home, which may be in a remote village; he considers it a duty to send home part of his savings. If his wife cannot live with him where he works, he leaves her in the care of the joint family. Children are looked after by aunts and grandmothers as well as mothers, and old people do not lack a family to care for them.

From the first, as a sign of respect, boys touch the feet of both parents, and girls touch the feet of their mothers; the relationship symbolized by this gesture continues for as long as the older persons are alive. To the last, the senior man of the family is regarded as head.

Marriages are arranged for a boy and girl by their parents, and until recently the choice of partners was severely restricted by caste. Within such limits, the choice was governed by spiritual affinity, and parents still consult an astrologer to find whether a proposed couple are suited. This probably goes back to a time when a seer would give real psychological advice about a union, and some of the advice still offered may have a certain value. Parents do consult their children's wishes as well, but many young people rely on the judgment of their elders, who are experienced in the kind of life they expect to lead.

A man working away from home may prefer to let his parents choose a girl for him from a neighbouring family. He will then, if he can, go back to his home village for the wedding, or else the bride will travel to him.

In the past, some Hindu families considered it so important to get their daughters married to good husbands that they arranged marriages for them at a very early age—even four or five—and paid large dowries to the bridegroom's family. In 1955 the minimum age for marriage was fixed by the law of the Republic of India at eighteen for boys and fifteen for girls, and the dowry system is now banned, though some families get round the law.

After the wedding, which takes place at the bride's home, the bridegroom brings her to his own home, and she becomes a member of his joint family. If he has to live away from home to work, he sometimes leaves

her in the care of his mother and other elders; the mother-in-law is a
very important person for a young Hindu wife. In the days of child
marriages, the bride sometimes stayed at her parents' house until she
was old enough to join her husband.

Hindu statements about the status of women give them an exalted place.
The Vedas call a wife the 'bliss-giver' of the family. The ancient
legendary law-giver Manu even decreed that women should be treated as
goddesses; he says:

> Where women are worshipped, the gods are pleased;
> where they are not worshipped, religious acts are fruitless.

(Manu, III, 56)

The role of the Hindu mother in Britain is different from the role of
the Hindu mother in India, where housework, especially cooking, is very
time-consuming. In Britain the Hindu mother often goes to work to earn
money for the family. She gets up very early in the morning, and prepares breakfast for the family. She prepares a packed lunch for her
husband and sometimes for her children, although most Hindu children
stay to school dinners. If her husband works at night, he may say that
he will get his own meal after he has had a rest. When the wife comes
back from work she prepares and clears away the evening meal.

Hindu women run the home and control it completely. The average Hindu
man has little say in the home and does not help very much in the house,
even when his wife is at work. Hindus admire and respect a woman who
looks after the family well, does the shopping thriftily, cooks meals
on time and still has time to join in the fun they have together. Hindu
women enjoy cooking, and not only buy food from shops owned by Indians
but also buy British food from supermarkets.

Most Hindus are vegetarians, and many do not even eat eggs; the rules
vary with different regions and castes. Food is simple during the week;
at the weekend, when the wife may have more time and guests are often
entertained, meals are more elaborate and there are more dishes to choose
from. Rice and vegetables are the main part of the diet. Protein is
largely provided by pulses—peas, beans, lentils (also called dāl) and
chick-peas (also called gram). Milk is drunk warm, with sugar. Curd
(yoghurt) is eaten with rice and used in cooking; ghee, which is butter
clarified by boiling away its water content, is also used in cooking,
especially for making sweets. Vanaspati, which resembles ghee but is
made from vegetable oils, is also used. Traditional food is very important to Hindus because it provides a link with their homeland.
Sweet food is important, especially at weddings, births and other festive occasions. On the other hand, it is avoided after funerals, and
a person whose relative has recently died will not accept sweet food if
it is offered to him (see 2.1.2, p. 27). Tact is needed in offering
people food; a person may refuse certain foods not just out of polite-
ness, but because someone has died or because he has taken a vow of
abstinence.

Many Hindus, as well as many other Asians, take off their shoes on
entering the home; they want to avoid bringing in dirt from outside,
and they feel more comfortable in bare feet or slippers than in heavy
outdoor shoes. Non-Hindus should be careful to do the same if they are
entering a home where this is customary.

The kitchen and dining room are the most important rooms, and great care is always taken when food is prepared or eaten; the next most important is the room for receiving visitors.

The Hindu kitchen in India is a place of great purity and piety; no-one would enter it without taking off their shoes and having a bath, even if they wear shoes in other parts of the house (see also 2.1.1). The shrine of the gods is often in the kitchen, and the food is offered to the gods there before being served to the family. In Britain the rules about the kitchen are less strict.

Some homes have an important periodical visitor: the purohita, the brahmin who performs samskāras (see 2.1.2) and other rituals. Some-times he may be invited to conduct worship at the household shrine, or to recite religious texts. He may also be the guru under whom the sons of the family are initiated (see 2.1.2). He may also be the family astrologer, giving advice on which days are the best for journeys or other enterprises, and casting the horoscopes of the children born in the family. This is a very exact and complicated art, because it requires knowledge of the position of the sun, moon, planets and stars not only on the date, but at the exact moment of birth. When the time comes to arrange a marriage, the astrologer will compare the horoscopes of prospective brides and bridegrooms to see if they will make a good match.

2.2.2. Caste

We can begin the study of caste by looking at purity and pollution. Everyone has some ideas of what is pure or clean and what is not; we keep them separate by washing our hands after touching what is unclean or before touching what is clean. Different people have different ideas of what is clean; ask round the class to find differences among the pupils.

Ideas of purity are strong among Hindus, and help to explain caste. Certain people are unclean because of their occupations: a sweeper because he handles dirt; a barber because hair is dead matter; a tanner or a butcher because he handles parts of dead animals. Other people have to keep clean, especially a priest, because he approaches the gods and handles sacred things.

Hindu family ties are so strong that pollution affects all members of a family. After a birth or a death, for example, all relatives have to go through a period of purification,because both birth and death cause pollution. Again, if some members of a family do polluting work, the whole family is polluted by it. Occupations therefore tend to run in families, not only as a way of handing on skills, but because people want to protect their families from pollution: a farmer's son does not want to be a tanner, and a priest's son does not want to be a farmer. For the same reason, Hindus marry people of similar occupation and way of life.

A caste is a group of people marked off from others by rules of purity, usually marrying only within the caste, and usually having a hereditary occupation.

In the village, caste serves to assign people to particular occupations; it thus ensures a supply of workers for all jobs. The castes co-operate with each other by providing goods, services and employment. A person looks to his caste for leadership, support, help in need, and also marriage partners for his children.

A 'high' caste is a caste that is considered purer than others; a 'low' caste is impure. The villagers can tell which castes are high, because they will not receive cooked food from lower castes; from very low castes they will not receive even raw food or water. Some castes will not eat with lower castes, and some are so low that others will not touch them: these are called untouchables, depressed castes, scheduled castes or Harijans ('God's people'). They often live in a separate part of the village, and use separate wells. They are the poorest and least educated group in India, and generally do the dirtiest work, although the Government tries to help them to gain education and better jobs.

There are many hundreds of castes in India, but as each caste is re-stricted geographically, there are only a few in each village. A typical village contains from a dozen to twenty, including brahmins, potters, weavers, tanners, barbers and sweepers (an untouchable caste), to pro-vide all the services needed for the functioning of the community. There is usually a dominant caste which includes the wealthier peasants, though many of its members may be poor.

The brahmins are a group of particularly pure castes; they need to be pure because they perform rituals for others, and preserve the Veda and other sacred texts. Some castes, however, have non-brahmin priests.

The Sanskrit literature of Hinduism was mainly composed by brahmins, so it reflects their point of view. It says that there are four groups of people, called the four varnas: brahmins who are holy and learned men, kshatriyas who are kings and warriors, vaishyas who are farmers and merchants, and shūdras who have to serve the others. This theory occurs first in a Vedic hymn (*Rig-Veda*, X, 90; see Zaehner, *Hindu Scriptures*, 10), where the functions of the four varnas, and their relation to each other, are expressed mythologically: the brahmins come from the mouth of the original man, the kshatriyas from his arms, the vaishyas from his thighs and the shūdras from his feet. The first three of the four varnas are called Aryans or Twice-born—that is, they are allowed to take part in Vedic rituals (see 2.1.2). The shūdras are non-Aryan; they are the majority of Hindus. The Sanskrit books also say that the castes originated from intermarriage between the four varnas. The varnas are sometimes called the four castes, but this is misleading as there are really hundreds of castes. Modern Hindu writers often defend the varna system as a natural and useful division, while condemning the com-plexities and privileges of caste.

Protest against caste, especially against the privileges of brahmins, is old. Buddhist texts often criticize and ridicule the brahmins, and the bhakti cults teach that all devotees are equal. Gāndhī campaigned against untouchability. From 1956 onwards, many untouchables became Buddhists in protest against caste. Caste can be a burden to high as well as low castes; many modern brahmins have refused to keep up the rules of purity. On the other hand, caste promotes solidarity among people of the same occupation, even if they differ in wealth or edu-cation; in times of difficulty, one can turn to one's caste-fellows for help.

Modern city life—factory and office work, public transport, piped water, convenience foods, restaurants, constant contact with strangers—tends to weaken the rules of purity, and the Indian Constitution outlaws discrimination, but caste still survives. It is very important in marriage, and castes can also be powerful political and economic groups.

2.2.3. *Resources*

Ewan, *Understanding Your Hindu Neighbour.*
Kanitkar in Jackson (ed.), *Perspectives on World Religions.*
Killingley, 'What about caste?'
Mahadevan, *Outlines of Hinduism*, 69-75.
Mandelbaum, *Society in India.*
Mohanti, *My Village, My Life.*
Sharma, *Rampal and His Family.*
Srinivas, *Caste in Modern India.*

2.3. *THE GODS*

2.3.0. *Introduction*

It is impossible to say how many Hindu gods and goddesses there are; many of them are only known in particular regions, while often it is hard to say whether two groups of worshippers in different places are worshipping the same god in two different forms, or two different gods. Sometimes the worshippers of a local goddess, such as Ambā in Gujarat, will say that she is the wife of the great god Shiva, but at other times the same worshippers may treat her as an independent deity. Some ancient texts of the Vedic period say there are 33 gods; later texts sometimes say there are 330,000,000. Neither of these is meant to be an exact number; the point is that there are many gods.

But that does not mean that every Hindu worships countless gods. He may worship only one god, whose home is the village temple or a simple open-air shrine under a tree; or he may worship one supreme god and regard other gods as his assistants, to be worshipped on particular occasions.

So there is a difference between what we call 'God' with a capital G, which is the omnipotent lord of the universe, and what we call 'a god', which is any personal being that is worshipped. The former is called Īshvara ('Lord') in Sanskrit; the latter is called deva 'a god', or devī 'a goddess', or (to include both sexes) devatā 'a deity, a divinity'. Similar words are used in other Indian languages.

But if there is one God who is Lord of all, which of the many gods is he? There are many rival answers to this question. Some Hindu theological systems exalt one of the gods among the rest and call him Īshvara— 'the Lord' or 'God'—or Brahman; this idea is often expressed mythologically, by means of myths in which one or more gods pay homage to a particular god or appeal to him for help. Another way of answering the question is to say that none of the gods that people worship is supreme; the true God who is Lord of all is beyond our knowledge, and the gods are forms which He takes in order to be accessible to ordinary people. This unknowable God can also be called Brahman.

The *Bhagavadgītā* is a well-known example of a text which exalts a particular personality—Krishna—above all other gods. In the *Gītā*, Krishna speaks of himself as God, and says:

> Even those devotees
> Who worship other gods with faith
> Are really worshipping Me alone,
> Though not in the proper way.
> For of all acts of worship, I
> Am the enjoyer and lord.

(Bhagavadgītā, IX, 23-4)

Different texts exalt different gods over the others in this way. Different Hindus therefore take different gods as their chief object of worship or 'chosen deity' (ishta-devatā), according to region, family tradition and individual choice. Some Hindus offer daily pūjā to a group of five gods: Vishnu, Shiva, Ganesha, Pārvatī (Shiva's wife), and Sūrya (the sun). This practice is said to have been established by the theologian Shankara (2.7.3).

As with other aspects of Hinduism, there are innumerable local traditions about gods, and at the same time there is a fairly consistent tradition handed down in Sanskrit texts and taught by brahmins all over India—though even among Sanskrit texts some are better-known in some parts of India than in others. One striking difference between the oldest and most widespread Sanskrit texts and many of the local traditions is that in the former, male gods predominate, while in the latter, goddesses are often worshipped. This characteristic of the Sanskrit tradition can be traced back to the old Vedic religion in which nearly all the important deities were male; it is paralleled by the importance attached to the male line in Hindu ritual and society (2.1.2, 2.2.1). In communities less influenced by the Aryan tradition inherited from Vedic times (2.6.2), the worship of goddesses is important; this can be seen especially in Bengal and in South India, which are the regions furthest from the north-west, where Aryan culture first prevailed.

In teaching about the gods, it is better to aim at conveying what Hindus feel towards their gods rather than completeness of information. Attitudes to gods are conveyed by Hindus through the telling of myths, the making of images, forms of worship (2.1.1, 2.1.3, 2.1.4, 2.1.5), and devotional poetry (2.5.3).

2.3.1. *The principal gods of Hinduism*

The three gods who are most commonly named together are Brahmā, Vishnu and Shiva. They are called respectively the creator, sustainer and destroyer of the universe; for in Hindu thought God not only creates the universe, but sustains it in being, and then in course of time destroys it, and after a period of rest creates it again, in an endless cycle of cosmic days and nights (2.4.1).

Vishnu and Shiva each have a great following of worshippers. Worshippers of Vishnu, who are called Vaishnavas, claim that Vishnu is the real cause of the origin, continuance and destruction of the universe; for when the time comes for the world to begin, Brahmā grows from Vishnu's navel and begins the work of creation, and at the end of the world Shiva springs from Vishnu's brow and destroys it. So long as the world continues, Vishnu maintains it in being and protects it, and after the end of the world he sleeps until it is time for the next creation to begin, and so the cycle continues. Worshippers of Shiva, who are called Shaivas, say that Shiva is the cause of the world, and that Brahmā and Vishnu sprang from Shiva's right and left sides.

Sometimes Brahmā, Vishnu and Shiva are represented as one god with three faces; this is called the Trimūrti, the 'triple form', and sometimes it is also called the Hindu trinity.

Brahmā is something of an odd one out in this triad of gods, for unlike Vishnu and Shiva he has no following of worshippers of his own; in mythology he plays a less prominent part than the other two, and often has to appeal to one or other of them for help. Nor are his images as varied or as striking as those of Vishnu or Shiva. He does, however, appear as an attendant god in the temples of other gods, and his image is worshipped there. His name is a form of the word Brahman; in the Vedas he appears, under various names, as creator, lord of the sacrifice, and father of the gods. His wife is Sarasvatī, the goddess of speech, learning and music.

To perform his role as preserver of the world, Vishnu has to protect

Brahmā, showing three of his four
faces, holding a book, a string
of beads, a jar and a sacrificial ladle.

Sarasvatī playing the vīnā,
holding a string of beads
and a book, with her goose.

it from the attacks of demons or other disasters, and to do this he often
appears in the form of an *avatār* or avatāra. This word, which means
'descent', refers to a form taken for a time by a god, in order to perform some task for the benefit of the world. Ten avatārs of Vishnu are
usually listed; but besides these, many others are sometimes mentioned
in mythology, while many historical figures such as Chaitanya (2.7.5)
and Rāmakrishna (2.7.11) have been so revered as to be regarded as
avatars of Vishnu. The ten principal avatārs are:

1. The Fish, who rescued Manu, the ancestor of man, from a flood.
2. The Tortoise, who supported the churning stick when the gods and
    demons churned the ocean (2.3.2.1).
3. The Boar, who lifted up the earth on his tusks when it had been
    thrown into the ocean by a demon.
4. The Man-Lion, who rescued Prahlāda and killed his demon father
    (2.3.2.3).
5. The Dwarf, who defeated the demon Bali by taking three gigantic
    strides (2.1.5.4).
6. Parashurāma, who massacred the kshatriyas (warrior-kings) in a
    vendetta.
7. Rāma, the prince who was exiled to fulfil his father's promise, and
    killed the demon king Rāvana.
8. Krishna, the most popular of the avatārs, who is often worshipped
    as a god in his own right (2.3.2.5).
9. Buddha, who according to Hindu mythology was an avatār of Vishnu;
    some say that he came to protect animals by abolishing blood sacri-
    fice, but others say that he came to deceive the wicked by preaching
    false doctrines.
10. Kalkī, who will come at the end of the Kali age to punish the wicked
    and reward the good, after which the Krita age will begin again
    (2.4.1).

Vishnu's wife is Lakshmī, the goddess of wealth and good fortune.
In contrast to Vishnu's gentle and protective character, Shiva is an
unpredictable and sometimes terrible god. His mythology shows him as
uniting apparently contradictory qualities: he is both creator and
destroyer, kindly and terrible. His older name is Rudra; the name Shiva,
which means 'kind, auspicious, happy', was given to him to emphasize the
benign side of his character and turn away his wrath. He is associated
with death, poison and snakes, but can also be a saviour to his worshippers.
The wife of Shiva appears in many forms under many names. She is
called Pārvatī, meaning 'daughter of the mountain', because she is the
daughter of the Himalayan mountain range; Durgā 'inaccessible'; Umā;
Bhavānī; Chandikā 'fierce', and so on. Often she is simply called
Devī 'the Goddess'. In her most terrible form, in which she dances in
cremation grounds, drinks blood, and slays all beings including her husband Shiva, she is called Kālī 'black'. This is the form of the goddess
to which goats are sacrificed at the Kālīghāt temple in Calcutta; it
reminds us that life is unpredictable, often cruel, and inevitably ends
in death. But even in this form the Goddess, like Shiva, is benevolent
as well as cruel; her worshippers call Kālī 'mother', and pray to her
for release from the round of rebirths, since it is only by accepting
death and abandoning all reliance on this world, which is really a
great cremation ground, that we can be released. In Bengal, the Goddess

is commonly worshipped as Durgā; in Gujarat she is Ambā.

Shiva and his wife (who is usually called *Pārvatī* when her family relationships are spoken of) have two sons: Skanda or Kārttikeya and *Ganesha*. Skanda, the leader of the army of the gods, is mainly worshipped by the Tamils of South India, who also call him Subrahmanya or Murugan. Ganesha is worshipped everywhere, for he is the remover of obstacles and should therefore be worshipped at the beginning of any enterprise, including going on a journey, writing a book, and worshipping other gods. He is easily recognized, for he is short and fat and has an elephant's head; many stories are told about the origin of his strange shape (2.3.2.2).

Many gods besides these are worshipped and mentioned in mythology. Some are old gods worshipped in Vedic times, around 1,000 B.C.; among these Vedic gods, Indra the warrior is remembered as the king of heaven, Yama the ruler of the dead is god of death, and Varuna the guardian of truth is god of the ocean; Agni remains as god of fire, and Sūrya as god of the sun. Besides these, there are many local deities who have been worshipped since prehistoric times to protect the village community from harm.

2.3.2. *Myths of the gods*

The personalities of the gods are expressed in their myths and in their images; often the images show the exploits told in the myths, while the myths are used to explain features of the images (e.g. 2.3.2.2). The myths have been told many times over in different versions, in Sanskrit poetry (the *Mahābhārata* and Purānas, and early versions in the Vedas), in vernacular poetry, and in modern times in films; and in all ages they have existed unrecorded on the lips of story-tellers. Here are five examples.

2.3.2.1. *The Churning of the Ocean*

Although the gods are divine and powerful, they sometimes have to achieve their ends by harnessing the cunning of strong and clever demons. Thus the gods sometimes have to enter into deception in order to maintain balance in creation.

Once, the gods sought Vishnu's advice on how to deal with overweening demons who were causing a great deal of trouble. Vishnu advised them to get the demons to help them churn the ocean so as to obtain the elixir of immortality (amrita). At the same time, they must keep the elixir from the demons because the demons would misuse it. For unlike the gods, who understood that immortality meant a full life-span, after which even they themselves must perish, the demons thought of immortality as simply escape from death. If the elixir fell into the demons' hands, the whole balance of life, death, rebirth, and time itself would be upset. The demons, for instance, would use the elixir to revive the dead, who, in a natural state of affairs, would be merely the result of the end of certain life-spans.

The elixir was to be obtained as the final result of a great churning of the ocean. First, poison would come out of the ocean, followed by a number of precious objects. The gods must neither be afraid of the poison nor must they covet the precious objects following it. In this adventure, the gods would be helped by their own divinity, their wisdom, and their devotion to Vishnu, their leader. The demons would not have these

Vishnu resting on his seven-headed
snake on the ocean, holding a discus
(represented by a shining ring), a
club, a conch and a lotus.

Lakshmī rising from the ocean when it
was churned, with Airāvata, Indra's
elephant. Her hand showers coins,
as she is goddess of wealth.

advantages. Both gods and demons worked together in order to obtain
the elixir. They wrapped the divine serpent Vāsuki round the great
mountain Mandara, threw Mandara into the ocean, and began churning it
by using Vāsuki as the churning rope and Mandara as the churning rod,
in much the same way as an Indian housewife used to churn butter. But
in this case, the team of gods pulled one end of the serpent while the
team of demons pulled the other end, causing the great churning rod to
revolve back and forth. The great mountain was so heavy that Vishnu
himself had to take the form of a huge tortoise in order to support it
under the water so that the gods and demons would not be pulled by the
gigantic weight into the water.

When the poison from the ocean came out, everybody sheltered under
the great Shiva, who swallowed the poison to save the others. The
poison did not harm him, but merely coloured his throat blue, for he
had not been afraid and was acting out of compassion. Then treasure
after treasure was yielded up by the ocean, including the cow that
grants all wishes, the pure white horse Ucchaishravas, the white elephant Airāvata, who became Indra's mount, and the beautiful Lakshmī, who
freely chose Vishnu as her lord, disdaining all the rest, who were
courting her. After Lakshmī, the ocean produced wine. This the demons
took. Finally, the ocean yielded up the elixir, contained in a white
jar held in the hands of the Physician of the gods.

When the demons saw the elixir, they snatched it from its bearer and
tried to keep it for themselves. However, Vishnu assumed the form of
a beautiful and desirable woman called Mohinī (which means 'deceptive'),
who was really an illusion. The demons then fell to worshipping this
false form of Vishnu and offered their elixir up to her to divide among
them. She, who was really Vishnu, then took the jar from the demons
and fed the elixir from it only to the gods, thereby deceiving the
demons and giving the gods immortality.

2.3.2.2. *The Birth of Ganesha*

There are many stories concerning the birth of Ganesha, who is a very
important god in Hindu mythology, although he looks rather ridiculous,
having the head of an elephant and the body of a fat man. One version
has it that Pārvatī, the wife of Shiva, wanted very much to have a son,
but Shiva refused to grant her wish. Instead, he handed her a bit of
her own garment to hold against her breast as a child. However, this
inanimate article she miraculously brought to life by the force of her
love, thereby making Shiva jealous. In his jealousy, he looked at
Pārvatī's beautiful son, and the boy's head fell off. Pārvatī was
inconsolable at her child's death, and in the end Shiva had to help
restore the child to life in order to make her happy again. He sent
his attendant, the bull Nandī, to bring back the head of the first
living creature he could find. This turned out to be an elephant's
head, which was put on the boy's body, and brought him to life again.

Since he was no longer beautiful and had undergone so much suffering,
Brahmā granted him a specially important position as a god, thus consol-
ing both the boy and his mother, Pārvatī. He was to be worshipped
before all other gods except Shiva and was to be known as Ganesha
(Ruler of the hosts) because Brahmā had made him the ruler of the hosts
of all the gods. So to this day, Hindus pay their respects to Ganesha,
invoking his name before undertaking tasks as diverse as writing a book,

Ganesha, the elephant-headed lord of obstacles. He
holds an elephant driver's goad, a noose, a cake which
he sniffs, and one of his tusks, which has broken off.
The animal he rides on is a rat.

Shiva dancing on a defeated demon, holding a drum
and a flame. His raised hand means 'Do not fear';
by pointing to his foot he invites his worshippers
to take refuge at his feet.

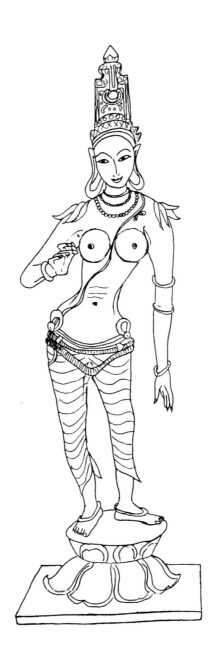

Pārvatī, wife of Shiva.

travelling, and making a business transaction.

There are also several explanations of why Ganesha has a broken tusk, which he holds in his hand. One is that when Nandī fought with the elephant to get its head, he broke one of its tusks; another is that when the sage Vyāsa composed the *Mahābhārata* he dictated it to Ganesha, who broke off a tusk to use as a pen.

2.3.2.3. *Prahlāda*

Prahlāda is known for his supreme devotion to Lord Vishnu. Prahlāda was born the son of Hiranyakashipu, a demon who had once, in an earlier incarnation, been a divine door-keeper of Vishnu.

In Hinduism it is possible for anyone to develop power, even over the gods, by means of certain physical and mental exercises. Such power should not be misused, but this was exactly what Hiranyakashipu did. He trained himself to achieve so much power that he was able to compel Brahmā himself to grant him certain favours, including these ways of avoiding death: no creature created by Brahmā would be able to kill Hiranyakashipu; death would not occur while Hiranyakashipu was inside or outside a house, by day or by night, while he was on the ground or in the air; no weapon could kill him, and he would be unharmed by men, animals, gods, demons, serpents, or anything which was animate or inanimate. Soon Hiranyakashipu became a truly terrible demon-king.

In spite of being Hiranyakashipu's son, Prahlāda was all that Hiranyakashipu was not: he was the soul of truth, and devoted to Vishnu. As a result, Hiranyakashipu hated this particular son, especially when Prahlāda told his father that devotion to Vishnu was the best thing he had learnt in his studies. Hiranyakashipu tried to kill his son, but was unable to do so because of Prahlāda's meditation on Vishnu. For devotion to truth is believed to protect one against harm, and Prahlāda's selfless devotion to Vishnu and truth was stronger than his father's self-acquired power.

Prahlāda told his father that his real enemy was his rebellious mind, and that he should turn to Vishnu, who was everywhere. This enraged Hiranyakashipu even more, so he struck at a pillar with his sword to prove that Vishnu could not be everywhere, or he would be in that pillar. It was then dusk. To his horror, Vishnu emerged from the pillar in the form of a creature that was half-man, half-lion. This Man-Lion avatar of Vishnu dragged Hiranyakashipu to the threshold, threw him across his knees, and killed him by tearing him open with his claws.

Thus Hiranyakashipu met his death without any of the favours granted by Brahmā being violated: it was twilight; his death had occurred at a threshold while he was suspended on the Man-Lion's knees; the Man-Lion had not used a weapon to inflict death, and in that form, Vishnu was neither god, demon, man, serpent, nor beast; and as Vishnu was both the inanimate pillar and the animate Man-Lion, the death-dealer was neither animate nor inanimate.

At Hiranyakashipu's death, there was great rejoicing, in which Prahlāda joined with a long hymn of praise to Vishnu. Vishnu, pleased with his devotee, asked him to name a favour. Prahlāda refused to do this as favours were only desired by those who were after worldly things. However, Prahlāda asked Vishnu for two things: first, that no desire grow in his heart; and second, that his father be purified of his sins.

These things Vishnu granted, and, acknowledging Prahlāda as his ideal
devotee, helped Hiranyakashipu eventually to be reborn as a god again.

2.3.2.4. *The Descent of the Ganges*

As we saw in the story of Prahlāda above, Hindus believe that mortals
can acquire great power by ascetic practices such as fasting, exposure
to heat and cold, and various other forms of self-discipline. They can
also acquire power by performing rituals, especially the most powerful
of all rituals, the horse-sacrifice, in which a horse has to be allowed
to roam for a year before it is killed. There are many myths about
people who gained so much power, either by asceticism or by sacrifices,
that they rivalled the gods.

Once upon a time, King Sagara, who was an ancestor of Rāma, acquired
so much power both by asceticism and by sacrifices that the gods began
to fear him. He needed only to perform one more horse-sacrifice before
he could become more powerful than the gods. Indeed, the sacrificial
horse was all ready and King Sagara himself initiated for this last
important sacrifice. In desperation, the gods stole the horse and hid
it in the hermitage of the sage Kapila.

Now, once a person has been initiated for a sacrifice, he is unable
to do anything else until that sacrifice has been completed. So King
Sagara was unable to go and recover the horse himself. However, as a
result of earlier ascetic practices, King Sagara had been rewarded with
sixty thousand sons, who had been miraculously borne to him by his queen,
Sumati. These sons were now sent by the king throughout the whole world
to find the stolen horse. The king remained behind with his only grandson, Amshuman, and continued his preparations for sacrifice.

King Sagara's sons dug up the whole world in their search, doing great
damage and killing demons, snakes and even gods in the process. Finally
they came to the hermitage of the sage Kapila and saw the stolen horse
grazing nearby. Without any thought of the respect and courtesy due to
a sage, these rash sons of the king rushed at Kapila, accusing him of
being a horse-thief. With angry disdain, Kapila merely looked at them
and reduced them all to a great heap of ashes by his fiery gaze.

After a long time, King Sagara grew anxious and sent his dear grandson
Amshuman to look for his uncles and the stolen horse. Amshuman found
his uncles' ashes, and weeping over them, wished to purify them with
water, but could not find any. Then the sacred bird Garuda, his maternal
uncle, addressed him from afar and told him that only the holy waters
of the Ganges could purify those ashes. So Amshuman returned home with
the horse and told King Sagara what Garuda had said. King Sagara,
mourning for his sons, completed his horse-sacrifice, but even he could
not bring the heavenly Ganges down to earth to purify the ashes of his
sons.

When King Sagara died, Amshuman became king and undertook the task of
bringing the sacred Ganges down to earth, but despite practising asceticism over thousands of years, he was unsuccessful, and eventually died.
His son, King Dilīpa, carried on this task, also for thousands of years,
and also died without achieving his aim. His son, Bhagīratha, became
king.

Bhagīratha was wise and virtuous and he, too, decided to carry on the
task of bringing about the descent of the Ganges. Leaving his kingdom
in the care of his ministers, for to his sorrow he had no heir,

Bhagīratha went to a holy place to practise asceticism. He lifted up
his arms, controlled his senses, stood in the midst of five fires in
the hottest season, and ate only once a month. These practices he
carried out for a thousand years. Then Brahmā became pleased with
Bhagīratha and granted him a double boon—that he would have an heir and
that the Ganges would descend to earth. However, Brahmā warned him that
when the Ganges descended, none but Lord Shiva would be able to sustain
the weight of her waters, for the earth would be crushed by her powerful
impact.

So Bhagīratha worshipped Shiva for a whole year, standing on the tip
of one toe, his arms uplifted, living on air, unsupported and yet
immobile. Finally Shiva was moved to receive the descent of the Ganges
on his head. The holy Ganges fell on Shiva's forehead, was imprisoned
in his hair, and finally let loose in a lake which divided into seven
streams. The seven streams divided further into other rivers that
flowed all over the earth (for all the rivers of the world are descended
from the heavenly Ganges), purifying all evil and death wherever they
flowed. King Bhagīratha led the Ganges to the sea, where at last the
ashes of his ancestors were purified; and so the sons of King Sagara
finally attained moksha.

2.3.2.5. *Krishna*

The Krishna legend consists of many different stories, some of which are
recounted here. There are many similarities between the Krishna legend
and the Christ story which we should treat as coincidences rather than
trying to identify the two. Krishna is the most important incarnation
(avatar) of Lord Vishnu. By the decree of Brahmā, he was born to save
the world from demons in the form of arrogant kings. He was miraculously
born at Mathurā to Princess Devakī and Prince Vasudeva, who were being
held prisoners by the wicked King Kamsa, one of these demons, who in
some versions was the nephew of Devakī, and in others her brother.
This was because it had been foretold that Devakī's eighth child would
one day kill Kamsa. Already, six of Devakī's children had been killed
by the orders of Kamsa. However, Krishna and his elder brother escaped
death by being miraculously transferred to Gokula ('cow-village'), where
they were brought up as cowherds. Thus Krishna became the foster-child
of simple peasants, Nanda and his wife Yashodā. It was in Gokula, in
fact, that Krishna was named by the family priest. The name means
'black', and we often see Krishna depicted in paintings as a black or
blue-black god. Krishna is also known as Govinda ('finder of cattle').

Various divine doings of Krishna are told here and there. In childhood, some of these doings took the form of impish escapades which
bewildered his foster-mother, Yashodā. One day, she scolded him for
swallowing earth; but when she looked into his open mouth to find the
earth, she saw the whole universe in it and had to worship him as God.
On another occasion, she wanted to punish Krishna for stealing her
butter, by tying him to a heavy mortar used for grinding spices. At
first she was unable to catch hold of him and tie him, for God has no
dimensions, neither an inside nor an outside, neither right nor left,
neither front nor back. But at last, in pity, Lord Krishna allowed
Yashodā to catch him and tie him up.

Krishna grew up with cowherds and cowherd girls as his companions.
One story about this part of his life tells us how he overcame a wicked

Krishna milking a cow while she licks her calf.

serpent called Kālīya, who had been polluting a river which had
poisoned Krishna's companions. In an ensuing battle with Kālīya,
Krishna leapt on to the serpent's hood, dancing on it and tormenting
the serpent so much by his divine weight that Kālīya had to beg his for-
giveness, involuntarily becoming a Krishna-worshipper because his head
had been touched by Krishna's divine feet. Krishna's friends were saved
and the serpent ordered to leave the river for the sea. The image of
Krishna dancing on the hood of a serpent is familiar to Krishna-
worshippers.

We are perhaps familiar with the devotional motif of a young girl
seeking her lover as a way of representing the devotee's search for
God. For instance, Roman Catholic nuns are known as 'brides of Christ'
and are given a ring to show their mystical marriage to Christ. The
Church is sometimes called the Bride of Christ. In much the same way,
this aspect of the devotee's relationship to Krishna as God is depicted
in stories concerning his early manhood, often shown in paintings of
Krishna dancing, fluting, and making love to cowherd girls (gopīs).
Krishna's love for the gopīs is God's divine love for the soul; his
flute music, which tempts the gopīs to leave their husbands and homes
for him, symbolizes God's voice, which calls the worshipper to leave
off worldly things for him. The gopīs become the mystical brides of
Krishna, the most favoured of them being Rādhā, who is often depicted
with him in paintings. However, he has to teach the gopīs that it is
not physical nearness which is of prime importance in their love and
worship of him. Once, when they were filled with personal pride in his

Krishna and Rādhā.

love, he disappeared from them, even from Rādhā, his most ardent
devotee. It was only when they began to call his name over and over,
imitate his gestures and dancing (thinking of him so much that they saw
no difference between themselves and him), meditate on him and sing his
praises, that he reappeared to sing and dance with them. Krishna
worshippers today express their longing for Krishna in the same way,
and re-enact the songs and dances of the gopīs as part of their devotion
(bhakti).

After many adventures, Krishna returned to his birthplace of Mathurā,
and, as earlier prophesied, killed his wicked relation, King Kamsa. He
then freed both his parents, Prince Vasudeva and Princess Devakī, restor-
ing the kingdom to his maternal grandfather. In his new elevated role
of prince, he had to say goodbye to his old companions, the cowherds
and cowherd girls of Gokula, in order to pursue his destiny as saviour
of the world in further adventures. However, he consoled them, his
weeping worshippers, by reminding them that they could never be separated
from him as long as they thought about him, imitated his actions, and
identified themselves with him.

In the great epic poem, the *Mahābhārata*, more adventures of Krishna
are recorded. He became the friend and counsellor of the five sons of
King Pāndu and preached the *Bhagavadgītā* to one of them, Arjuna, before
the battle which is the centre of that epic.

2.3.3. *Images of the gods*

The image is an important part of the way in which a Hindu experiences
the divine. For it is through an image that a god grants darshana,
which means 'sight': that is, the god appears in the form of the image
and allows the worshipper to see him, rather as a monarch allows himself to be seen by his subjects at a formal audience, a procession or
a garden party. It is also through the image that the worshipper can
express his devotion to the god by gestures, mantras and offerings
(see 2.1.1). Worshippers can have darshana in other ways also: they
can see the god in imagination; some saints such as Chaitanya and
Rāmakrishna have had visions of gods in bodily form; and many Hindus
long for nothing better after death than to see and serve their chosen
god for ever in heaven. But it is through the image that the form of
the god becomes familiar to the worshipper.

Hindus have great respect for images and pictures of all kinds. If
you cannot pay your respects to your father, your guru or a revered
political leader in person, you can put up a photograph of him and hang
a garland on it; images of the gods are regarded similarly. But images
in temples are treated in a special way: they have been through a ceremony called prāna-pratishthā, 'putting in the breath', in which the
god is called upon to place his life in the image. Before the prāna-
pratishthā, the image is only a thing; it can be bought and sold, stored
and carried like any other goods. But after the god's life has been
placed in it, it has to be worshipped daily. If an image cannot be
worshipped any more—for instance, if a temple is to be demolished, or
if a broken image is to be replaced by a new one—it cannot be thrown
away like an ordinary thing; it has to be thrown into the sea.

A Hindu, therefore, is not just a worshipper of wood and stone. He
treats an image with reverence if he can see that it represents a god,
in the same way as a person is represented by his photograph, because

in this way the god has been made available for him to worship. He
treats it with greater reverence if it has been consecrated with the
prāna-pratishthā ceremony, because then the people who set it up have
undertaken to ensure that the god will be worshipped in it daily.

A temple image may be of wood, clay, plaster, stone or metal; the most
striking ones are bronze, a material which allows the sculptor to give
the figure a lively pose and a variety of surface textures. For home
worship clay, wood and brass are used, and highly coloured pictures of
the gods are printed on posters and calendars.

For an image to be a representation of a particular god, it has to
have features by which the god can be recognized. The study of these
features is called iconography. Just as a study of Christian iconography will teach us to recognize an Annunciation or a Crucifixion, and
artists have to know iconography to produce acceptable Christian pictures, so a study of Hindu iconography will enable us to tell a Shiva
from a Vishnu, and Hindu artists have to know the rules of iconography
to produce a proper representation of a myth such as the churning of the
ocean or Krishna conquering Kālīya (2.3.2.1, 2.3.2.5).

Gods can be recognized by their dress, by what they hold in their
hands, and by the animals they ride on or are accompanied by. They are
often shown with four or more arms, which both shows their superhuman
power extending in all directions, and enables the artist to place more
than two attributes in the god's hands. Any hands which are not holding
attributes may be used to convey messages to the worshipper through gestures. A hand held upwards with the palm forwards means 'Do not fear';
a hand held downwards with the palm forwards means that the god pours
out gifts; a hand pointing to the god's foot means that worshippers
should seek refuge at his feet.

Brahmā usually carries a jar and a ladle (both used in the old Vedic
ritual), a book—in the traditional Indian form of a sheaf of oblong
leaves—to represent the Vedas, and a string of beads. He has four
faces, because he faces in all directions, and a pointed beard. He
rides on a goose (often called a swan in English, to avoid the undig-
nified associations of the word 'goose'). His wife Sarasvatī also rides
a goose and carries a book, and she plays on a vīnā, the long-necked
Indian lute.

Vishnu has a tall, cylindrical head-dress, and carries a conch, a
discus, a club and a lotus, or sometimes a bow. Before the creation of
the world he reclines on a seven-headed snake, floating in the ocean;
sometimes he is shown at the beginning of creation, with Brahma rising
from a lotus flower which grows from Vishnu's navel. He is usually blue
in colour, and wears the fork-shaped forehead mark worn by Vaishnavas
(2.1.1). He rides on a mythical bird, Garuda. His wife Lakshmī is
shown standing on a lotus, rising from the ocean when it was churned
(2.3.2.1).

Vishnu's avatārs are also blue. Rāma carries a bow, and is often
seen with his wife Sītā, his brother Lakshmana, and his ally the monkey
Hanuman, who is also sometimes worshipped as a god. Krishna often holds
a flute. There are many exquisite paintings of his adventures among the
cowherds, painted in the eighteenth century in north-west India.

In a temple of Shiva, the main centre of worship is usually not a
figure of the god but a linga. The linga is Shiva's phallus; some of
the myths about Shiva make this clear, and so do some sculptured lingas;

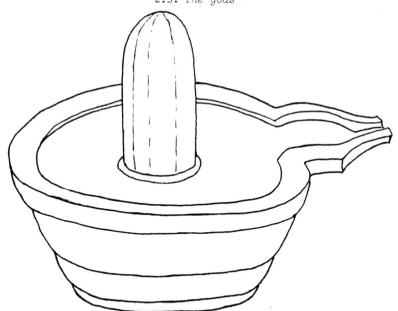

A linga, the form in which Shiva is usually
worshipped. Water is poured on the top and carried
away by the channel surrounding the linga.

but there is no need to mention this in teaching, and indeed the significance of the linga is so manifold that it could be positively misleading to draw attention to its phallic aspect. The linga is a
manifestation of Shiva's energy; it is sometimes described in myths as
a column of fire. What matters most to worshippers is that the linga
is the form in which Shiva condescends to receive worship. In the
temple it has the form of a round-topped cylinder of stone, rising out
of a circular dish which has a spout coming out of its southern side
(the right-hand side as you look eastwards into the temple shrine);
this stands on a plinth, so that the top of the linga is about two feet
above the floor. The linga is the cultic centre of the temple, directly
under the top of the spire, and represents the centre of the world. In
worship, water is poured over the linga to wash it, and is carried away
by the spout; flowers and leaves are placed on it, and food offerings
and āratī are made to it as to the images of other gods. Small lingas
of stone, brass or clay are kept in houses.
    Shiva is also represented in human form in many types of image. He
has a pile of tangled hair rising in a cone on his head, and in it are
the moon, and the river Ganges; for when the Ganges first descended from
heaven, its fall would have shattered the earth if Shiva had not caught
it in his hair first (2.3.2.4). He has a third eye in the middle of his
forehead. His throat is blue, stained by the poison he drank to save
the world at the churning of the ocean (2.3.2.1), and he has a cobra
round his neck. He is dressed in the skin of a deer, or sometimes a
tiger or an elephant—trophies of beasts he has killed. He carries a

trident and other weapons. Sometimes he appears in a calm pose, standing or sitting with his wife Pārvatī; but the most famous theme in Hindu
sculpture is Shiva dancing, holding a drum and a flame, and surrounded
by a ring of flames representing the world, with one hand raised in the
'Do not fear' position and another pointing to his foot as a refuge
from the dangers of the world.

Shiva rides on a bull, Nandī, who often appears in Shaiva temples,
sitting outside the shrine and facing the linga. In mythology, Nandī
is Shiva's door-keeper.

Of Shiva's sons, Skanda is an agile young man; he carries a spear and
rides a peacock. Ganesha is a complete contrast: he is fat, usually
seated, and has an elephant's head. There are many accounts of how he
came by this shape (2.3.2.2). He usually carries a cake in one hand,
and sniffs it with his trunk. He also carries one of his tusks which
has broken off, an elephant-driver's goad, and a noose; he rides on a
rat.

The Goddess, Shiva's wife, appears in many forms by herself. She is
often shown killing a buffalo-demon (2.1.5.3); in this form she is
called Durgā, and rides on a lion or sometimes a tiger. She carries
a trident like Shiva, also a sword and a bow, and a discus like Vishnu.
As Kālī, her terrible form, she is dark blue or black, and wears
severed heads and arms; she dances wildly on the lifeless body of
Shiva, for he is powerless without her.

Nandi, Shiva's bull, decorated with chains and bells.

2.3.4. *Learning about the gods*

The myths and images of the gods provide plenty of opportunity for imaginative work. Here are some suggestions as to what a class can do.

Learn to recognize Brahmā, Vishnu, Shiva, the Goddess and Ganesha by the things they hold or wear; read the stories which explain these things (Shiva's tiger skin or elephant skin from demons that he killed; Ganesha's elephant head and broken tusk). Learn to recognize images showing particular exploits of the gods: Shiva dancing, the Goddess killing the buffalo-demon, Brahmā growing out of Vishnu's navel to create the world. Draw your own images.

Read the story of Krishna (in Thomas, *Epics, Myths and Legends of India*, or in more detail in Archer, *The Loves of Krishna*, or Raghavan, *The Indian Heritage*). Learn to recognize pictures or images of Krishna dancing on Kālīya; Krishna stealing butter; Krishna dancing with the cowherd girls. Krishna-līlā 'the play of Krishna' is a popular form of entertainment; the performers can do what they like so long as they follow some part of Krishna's story. The class can do its own Krishna-līlā; there is plenty of opportunity for dancing, music, mime and fighting.

Read the story of Rāma (in Boothalingam, *The Children's Ramayana*, in Thomas, *Epics, Myths and Legends of India*, or in more detail in Dutt's translation, or Raghavan, *The Indian Heritage*). Learn to recognize images of Rāma, Sītā, Lakshmana and Hanuman. Discuss the religious ideas in the story: how Rāma faces misery to avoid making his father's word false, showing the sanctity of duty and truth; how Sītā, Lakshmana and Hanuman show their devotion to Rāma.

The images and myths can be used as stimuli for art work and imaginative writing.

2.3.5. *Resources*

Archer, *The Loves of Krishna*.
Basham, *The Wonder That Was India*, 300-322.
Boothalingam, *The Children's Ramayana*.
Devi, *Gods and Goddesses in Indian Mythology*.
Dutt, *The Ramayana and the Mahabharata*.
Ions, *Indian Mythology*.
Mitchell, *Hindu Gods and Goddesses*.
Narayan, *Gods, Demons and Others*.
O'Flaherty, *Hindu Myths*.
Raghavan, *The Indian Heritage*.
Stutley, *A Dictionary of Hinduism*.
Thomas, *Epics, Myths and Legends of India*.

Hindu Iconography Pack.
Hinduism: Goddesses and Minor Gods and *Hinduism: The Three Great Gods* (leaflets).
Hinduism Slide Sets.

Photographs of images or paintings can be found in the books by Thomas, Ions, Basham and Archer, and in books on Indian art. Devotional posters and small images can be bought from Indian art shops or Indian bookshops (4.3), or borrowed from Hindu homes.

2.4. *HINDU IDEAS*

2.4.0. *Introduction*

Hinduism as a whole has no fixed creed, although some Hindu sects have
very definite systems of doctrine which have been laid down by their
teachers, and in some cases supported by elaborate philosophical arguments. Hinduism has a long tradition of theological debate, in which
each school went on elaborating its arguments to strengthen them
against the arguments of opposing schools—not only Hindu, but Buddhist
and Jain schools. In modern times, Hindu writers argue against materi-
alism and Christianity.

The outline presented here concentrates on those beliefs which are
common to most Hindu sects; some of these beliefs are also shared by
Buddhism, Jainism and Sikhism.

2.4.1. *Some fundamental Hindu ideas*

Karman means 'action' and also the way in which action shapes one's
destiny. Good or bad fortune is the result (or 'fruit') of previous
good or bad karman. Since we have been born countless times before,
and most of us will be born many times again, our present fortune,
including our status at birth and the fact that we happen to be human
rather than animals or gods, is the fruit of actions in previous births,
and our actions now may not bear fruit until a later birth. This
explains apparently undeserved good or evil fortune.

Rebirth as described above is accepted as a fact of life, by Buddhists,
Jains and Sikhs as well as Hindus. One may be reborn as a person, an
animal or even a plant in this world, or in one of the many heavens and
hells, according to one's good or evil deeds. After a period in a
heaven or hell, one may be reborn again in this world; one cannot
remain in heaven or hell for ever, since however many good or evil
deeds one has done, they can only earn a certain amount of bliss or
pain. Hindus do not see how Christians can expect eternal reward or
punishment for the deeds of only one life.

The heavens and hells, as well as this world, are part of the round
of existence (*samsāra*). Samsāra is beginningless and endless, and
although sometimes enjoyable it is on the whole evil. Release from it
(moksha) is the Hindu idea of salvation.

The universe comes into existence and is destroyed, over and over
again; time is cyclic. It is not created out of nothing, and when it
is destroyed it does not become nothing; creation merely brings the
dormant universe into activity, and the periodical destruction merely
makes it inert and formless again.

Within the cycle of creation and destruction is a shorter cycle of
four ages (yuga). In the first age, the world is perfect; at the end
of each age it declines. We are now in the last and worst of the four—
the Kali age (the name has nothing to do with the goddess Kālī). In the
Kali Yuga unrighteousness prevails and most brahmins do not follow their
duties; the idea that we are now living in the Kali age corresponds to
the Christian doctrine of the Fall. The Kali age began with the war
described in the *Mahābhārata*, in 3,102 B.C. according to traditional
chronology; it lasts for 432,000 years, so it still has well over four
thousand centuries to run. As far as the historical past and the

foreseeable future go, then, we are always in the Kali age. At the end
of the Kali age, the wicked will be destroyed and the first age will
begin again. The cycle of four ages takes 4,320,000 years; when it has
happened a thousand times, a cosmic day will be over, and the world
will be destroyed. After a cosmic night, lasting another 4,320,000,000
years, it will be created again. The time-scale of samsāra is so vast
that even the gods eventually pass away, to be reborn as other beings;
likewise other beings can be reborn as gods (2.3.2.3).

In this world, man has three aims:

dharma 'righteousness, fulfilment of the sacred law'
artha 'success, profit, political power'
kāma 'pleasure, desire'

He should not, however, pursue a lower aim at the expense of a higher
one. To pursue dharma is to perform good karman; by doing so, one
ensures good fortune, including good future births, perhaps in heaven.
A person's dharma is determined by various factors—for instance, his
caste.

Beyond these three worldly aims there is a fourth aim, *moksha* or
salvation. Moksha is an eternal state; it is therefore quite different
from heavenly existence, which has to come to an end. Moksha is not
achieved by deeds, like the other three aims, but by knowledge: knowledge of the eternal truth which is different from the fleeting things
of samsāra. What that truth is, and how it can be known, differs from
school to school; but it is generally agreed that moksha is knowledge
of *Brahman*.

Brahman is the highest truth, the eternal being on which all other
beings depend. It is conscious, and our ability to be conscious of our
surroundings shows that within our bodies there is a *self (ātman)*
which is of the same nature as Brahman, or even identical with Brahman.
Brahman is also the highest bliss: it is free from all suffering, and
to know Brahman is to be released from samsāra into the infinite bliss
of moksha. The three words Being, Consciousness, Bliss (sat, chit,
ānanda) sum up the nature of Brahman. Sometimes Brahman is seen not
just as an impersonal being but as God, with a personality known
through mythology.

Those who know Brahman perfectly reach moksha. Some say that this
knowledge can be achieved by *yoga*—which starts by training the body
and goes on to discipline the mind. Others say only a perfect understanding of the Veda, especially the Upanishads, can lead to knowledge
of Brahman. Others say that *bhakti* (devotion) to God can bring perfect
knowledge. In any case, such perfection can only be reached by long
striving which may last through many rebirths. The way to moksha is
often described as having three parts: action (karman), devotion
(bhakti) and knowledge (jnāna).

The idea of rebirth was familiar to the Buddha; he too taught a way
to moksha, and his sayings reflect a climate of ideas similar to that
of the Upanishads and *Bhagavadgītā*. Unlike them, however, he completely
rejected the authority of the brahmins and the Veda; this rejection
separates Buddhism from Hinduism.

Some of these ideas, especially karman, rebirth, dharma, bhakti, may
be introduced quite early; some mention of them will come up naturally
in the course of explaining and discussing stories. There is no need
to teach the Indian terms at that stage; what matters is that pupils

should be familiar with what Hindus understand by storing up good or
bad fortune for oneself by good or bad action, for instance, rather
than that they should know the word 'karman'. The words can come later
when the ideas have already taken some shape in the pupils' minds.

Yoga can also be introduced to teenagers by an experienced and sensitive teacher. A brief, practical lesson can be given without attempting
a real yoga course; pupils can try elementary postures and breathing,
and learn a few of the main ideas of yoga.   .

2.4.1.1. *Resources*

Basham (ed.), *A Cultural History of India*, 60-82.
Basham, *The Wonder That Was India*, ch. VII.
Butler, *Teaching Yoga*.
Mahadevan, *Outlines of Hinduism*.
Parrinder, *The Indestructible Soul*.
Sen, *Hinduism*.
Zaehner, *Hinduism*.

2.4.2. *Some varieties of Hindu doctrine*

The ideas described above are common to most kinds of Hinduism, but they
do not by themselves constitute a systematic body of doctrine. However,
various teachers have presented theological systems, and supported them
with arguments based both on the Hindu scriptures and on reason.

A system of this kind is called a darshana, a 'view' (the word can
also refer to the experience of seeing a god, 2.3.3). A darshana is
a way of viewing or looking at both this world and whatever is beyond
it, and includes both philosophy and theology. But Hindu thought does
not aim simply at a right way of seeing things; it aims at salvation
also, so that each system claims to teach the knowledge that leads to
moksha. From ancient times it has been customary to present such a
system, with arguments against opposing systems, in Sanskrit; some
systems, however, present their teaching in the vernacular languages of
India, and in modern times English has often been used.

The most widespread system or darshana is *Vedānta*. Vedānta, which
means 'the end of the Veda', is devoted to the interpretation of the
best-known part of the Veda, the Upanishads (2.5.1), which teach about
Brahman. Vedānta is concerned with the meaning of the term Brahman,
and its relation to the world and to the individual self; those who
truly know this reach moksha.

There are several schools of Vedānta, with different views of the
nature of Brahman, the self and the world, and of the relation between
them. The most influential of them is *Advaita* Vedānta, whose views
were formulated by the philosopher-theologian *Shankara* (8th century
A.D.;   2.7.3). Advaita Vedānta holds that Brahman is the only reality,
and that all differences are the result of false knowledge. If we could
rid ourselves of this false knowledge, we would see no difference
between Brahman and the world; all is Brahman, and there is no duality
(the word advaita means 'free from duality; non-dualist'). Freedom
from false knowledge is moksha.

It is easier to understand this if you think of Shankara's favourite
analogy of the snake and the rope. Suppose you see a rope in the dusk
and think it is a snake. When you discover that it is a rope, where
has the snake gone? If you try to show where it has gone, or where it

came from, you can only point to the rope. But the snake did not
emerge out of the rope, and it has not disappeared into it; it could not
have, because, as you now know, it never was anything other than the
rope. Yet, before you knew it was a rope, the snake was real enough to
frighten you. Brahman is like the rope: it is real, and it remains unchanged. The world is like the snake: it is not utterly unreal, but it
has no reality of its own, and once you know what reality underlies it,
you are free from it.

Since Advaita Vedānta recognizes no real difference between Brahman,
the self and the world, there would seem to be no place in it for devotion to God; but this is not so. In so far as the world is real, it
is caused and ruled by God; and devotion to God can bring us nearer to
the truth. However, since devotion implies a difference between the
worshipper and God, it cannot reveal the true nature of Brahman, which
is identical with the self.

While Advaita Vedānta thus treats the idea of God as an imperfect
version of the truth, other schools of Vedānta assert that God is absol-
utely real and identical with Brahman; they also think not of one self
but of a multitude of selves. *Rāmānuja* (12th century A.D.) identified
Brahman or God with Vishnu, who loves and saves all those who turn to
him. Rāmānuja held that while Brahman, the selves and the world were
one, the distinctions between them were not false but eternal and real.
He lived and taught in the Tamil region of South India, where devotion
to Vishnu had already been fostered by Tamil poetry. Another South
Indian, Madhva (13th century) held that Vishnu, the selves and the world
were three separate kinds of being. In Gujarat in Western India,
Vallabha (1481-1533) taught that Krishna was God, and that bhakti was
the only means of salvation; a similar doctrine was taught in 18th-
century Bengal by Baladeva, a follower of Chaitanya (2.7.5). Baladeva
held that since God's powers were beyond the reach of thought, all
theological arguments were useless. These other schools of Vedānta
are mainly known in particular regions; Advaita Vedānta, however, is
known all over India, and has therefore become the best-known in the
West.

Besides Vedānta, there are other systems of Hindu doctrine. In South
India, the Shaiva Siddhānta system teaches that Shiva is lord of the
world, and brings salvation to his devotees by removing the defects
which bind them to rebirth. Further north, the Lingāyats also hold
that Shiva is supreme; they reject the authority of brahmins, and give
more freedom than many other Hindu sects to women, permitting widow
remarriage. Tantrism, particularly strong in Bengal, uses the ancient
idea that the human body and personality correspond, in every detail,
with the universe; it aims at understanding this correspondence and so
gaining freedom. The *Swāminārāyana* sect was founded in the early nineteenth century by a Gujarati brahmin, Sahajānanda or Swāminārāyana
(1781-1830), whose followers consider him an incarnation of God. Their
code of conduct includes abstinence from alcohol, strict rules in sexual
matters, and submission to the authority of their gurus or religious
leaders, of whom the chief is the spiritual successor of Swāminārāyana.
They think of God in the form of Krishna. Some hundreds of Gujaratis
in Britain belong to this sect.

Hinduism thus tolerates a wide variety of doctrine. This does not
mean, however, that all Hindus are indifferent to doctrine; many

writers use forceful arguments to dismiss all views but their own, which
they claim is the only one leading to moksha.

2.4.2.1. *Resources*

Basham, *The Wonder That Was India*, 323-35.
Raju, *The Philosophical Traditions of India*.
Zaehner, *Hinduism*.

2.4.3. *Hindu ideas in the modern world*

Hindu ideas have always been changing, and their history is linked to
that of India (2.6). But, as in other countries, the political, economic and social changes brought by the nineteenth and twentieth centuries, including improved facilities for communication both within
India and with the rest of the world, have stimulated change.
  The British presence in India during these two centuries (2.6.5)
introduced new knowledge from outside India, and encouraged Indians
to take a fresh look at their own traditions, while printing, translation and education made the ancient texts more widely known. Partly
as a defence against missionaries and other critics, and partly in
response to the enquiries of sympathetic Westerners, Hindus in the
nineteenth century began to write and speak in defence of Hinduism—
rather than any particular Hindu school of thought—and to vindicate
what they considered to be the true Hinduism, sifting out what they
considered unworthy of it.
  In the early nineteenth century, *Rammohun Roy* (2.7.9) defended
Hinduism against missionary critics, and declared that the true
Hinduism was the worship of one formless God. He taught a new form of
Advaita Vedānta (2.4.2) influenced by Western rational theism: he saw
God, or Brahman, as the designer, maker and ruler of an ordered universe. The religious society he founded, the *Brāhmo Samāj*, brought
together many of the leading thinkers of nineteenth-century Bengal.
  Dayānanda Sarasvatī (1824-1883), a Gujarati brahmin, claimed that the
most ancient Sanskrit texts, the Vedas (2.5.1) were a revelation of
truth from God. The Vedas, he claimed, not only taught that there was
only one God, and laid down eternal rules of conduct, but contained
modern scientific ideas as well. He condemned polytheism and idolatry,
and said that God should be worshipped by the Vedic ritual of *homa* or
havan, in which fragrant substances are put in a fire while mantras
are chanted by the congregation. He pointed out that the Vedas do not
sanction the caste system with its hereditary privileges and disabilities
and held that the true brahmin was known by his character and learning,
not by his birth. He therefore urged that the caste system should be
replaced by a non-hereditary system of four varnas (2.2.2), to which
each person would be assigned according to his merits. He believed
that the West had brought nothing new to India; on the contrary, India
should preach the true religion to the world. In 1875 he founded the
Ārya Samāj, a movement to revive the ancient Vedic religion as he saw
it. The Ārya Samāj is particularly strong among Panjabi Hindus,
including those in Britian.
  The first Hindu of modern times to go overseas as a teacher of
Hinduism was Swāmī *Vivekānanda* (2.7.12). He regarded all religions as
approximations to the truth of Advaita Vedānta, which he thought was the
only religion compatible with modern science. Defending Hinduism against

the charge of lacking a concern for humanity, he founded an order of
sannyāsīs dedicated both to the teaching of Vedānta and to social
service. The Rāmakrishna Mission which he founded, and in which these
sannyāsīs have a leading role, has centres for teaching Hinduism in
India, Britain, the U.S.A., and elsewhere; it publishes books which
are available from the Rāmakrishna Vedānta Centre (4.3).

Gāndhī (2.7.14), who was brought up as a Vaishnava in Gujarat but without any deep understanding, first studied Hinduism seriously so that he
could explain it to European enquirers in London and South Africa, where
he was at the same time absorbing ideas from Ruskin, Thoreau, Tolstoy
and other writers, as well as from Christian and other Western friends.
He made some important Hindu ideas, especially those of non-violence and
the value of voluntary suffering, better known and respected both in
India and abroad. Tagore (2.7.13), a Bengali brahmin whose father was
a leading member of the Brāhmo Samāj, and *Rādhākrishnan*, a Telugu-
speaking brahmin from a traditional family, made Hindu views about the
nature of God and of man attractive to Western readers, and did much to
spread interest in Hinduism among them. Aurobindo Ghose (1872-1950),
a Bengali who had been sent to England for his education and returned
an Indian nationalist, sought to integrate Hindu ideas of the knowledge
of Brahman with modern evolutionary thought. He founded an ashram at
Pondicherry which now attracts followers from all over the world.

In the mid-twentieth century, airlines and the media have made
Hinduism far more familiar in the West than when Rammohun Roy or
Vivekānanda sailed to this country. Among the jet-age gurus, Bhakti
Vedānta Swāmī (1896-1977), a Bengali member of the Krishna-worshipping
sect founded by Chaitanya (2.4.2; 2.7.5) has brought the traditional
practice of dancing and chanting the names of Krishna to British streets,
through his International Society for Krishna Consciousness (ISKCON);
Guru Mahārāj Jī (1957-), through the Divine Light Mission, attracts
Western followers to the traditional Hindu practice of reliance on the
guru; and Mahārishi Mahesh Yogī has introduced a form of yoga involving
meditation on a mantra, under the new name of Transcendental Meditation.

Christianity has played an important part in modern Hindu thought;
many modern thinkers were educated at Christian schools and colleges,
and many of them have had a special reverence for Jesus, though without
giving him the unique place he holds in Christianity. Since the early
nineteenth century, when Christians often regarded Hinduism as totally
evil, many have taken a positive interest in Hinduism, learning Hindu
ways of thinking about God and man, or living as sannyāsīs.

2.4.3.1. *Resources*

Basham, *A Cultural History of India*, 365-82, 470-86.
Sarma, *Hinduism Through the Ages*.
Thomas, *The Acknowledged Christ of the Indian Renaissance*.

2.5. *HINDU LITERATURE*

2.5.0. *Introduction*

The most thorough way to study Hindu ideas is by reading Hindu texts. These vary greatly in length and difficulty, as well as in the extent to which they are known to Hindus. The reading of long passages from explicitly religious texts may be kept for the sixth form. But a few short passages from the sacred texts may be selected for younger pupils, and the teacher should look out for stories and poems which will appeal to children; a lot depends on how they are retold and presented by the teacher.

There is really no Bible of Hinduism, since different groups of Hindus in different regions read and recite texts in different languages. Certain texts are known all over India, but they are in Sanskrit, which only a few can understand; to most people they are known only by name, if at all, or only through popular versions in various languages. Furthermore, the view of the dharma texts is that the Veda, the most ancient and sacred part of Sanskrit literature, must be known only to a minority of Hindus, the Twice-born (2.1.2, p. 27). This restriction has been weakened in modern times by printing and education, which have made Vedic texts available to anyone in the original or in translation.

The texts which have been most influential, since the time of their composition in the last millennium B.C., are the Upanishads and *Bhagavadgītā*; in modern times they have become known to an increasing number of Hindus through translations in the vernacular languages and in English. The great variety of Hindu literature, coupled with the absence of a corpus of texts which all Hindus are expected to know, may be bewildering to the teacher. But it does give him some freedom to select for himself the texts that mean most to him and seem likely to mean most to the pupils; for a start, there are some useful anthologies: Alphonso-Karkala, *An Anthology of Indian Literature*; De Bary, *Sources of Indian Tradition*; Embree, *The Hindu Tradition*; Raghavan, *The Indian Heritage*.

2.5.1. *The Veda*

The *Veda* is the most ancient body of literature used by Hindus. It was built up in three main layers, from about 1200 B.C. to about 200 B.C. according to modern scholars; many Hindus believe it is much older, and ancient Hindu tradition says it is eternal. The three layers are:

(1) *Vedic Hymns*, used in worshipping the gods. Most of the old Vedic gods are largely forgotten today; the Vedic rituals are rarely practised, and most of the hymns are little known. But many of the hymns can be enjoyed as poetry or as speculative thinking on the cause of the universe. Certain *mantras* (verses) from the hymns are used in later ritual; the best-known is the Gāyatrī, used in the thread-ceremony and in daily prayers (2.1.1.1). The part of the Vedas containing the hymns is sometimes called the mantra portion, or the samhitā portion (samhitā means 'collection'). There are three main samhitās or collections of hymns: the Rig-Veda, containing hymns to the gods; the Yajur-Veda, containing verse and prose texts to be recited by the priest who carried out the ritual actions; and the

Sāma-Veda, containing hymns with tunes, for the use of a type of
priest who specialized in singing. There is a fourth Veda which is
not always included: the Atharva-Veda, containing magical spells
and prayers for cures and other personal benefits.

(2) *Brāhmanas*, prose texts which describe the Vedic ritual and discuss
its significance.

(3) *Upanishads*: dialogues and discourses in prose and verse. Their main
topics are the origin of the universe, the nature of man, life after
death, salvation (moksha) and Brahman. The Upanishads are the part
of the Veda which has had most influence on later Hindu thought; they
have also attracted Western thinkers since the beginning of the nineteenth century.

Selected hymns may be used, especially those that depend least on
mythological and ritual knowledge. As poetry, try the ones translated
by Basham (*The Wonder That Was India*, 400-405). Zaehner (*Hindu
Scriptures*) selects mainly from the speculative hymns; these can set
people thinking, especially the highly abstract *Rig-Veda*, X, 129.
O'Flaherty (*The Rig Veda*) chooses mainly those of mythological interest,
which require the reader to enter a world very different from his own,
and also from present-day Hinduism. Panikkar (*The Vedic Experience*)
selects from the whole Veda, and gives extensive comments.
The Brāhmanas are very long and difficult. A few mythological passages
from them are available in O'Flaherty, *Hindu Myths*; these are mainly
interesting as showing early forms of myths which are better-known in
later, fuller forms.
The Upanishads have a higher priority. Among them are dialogues in
which situation and character help to illustrate the teaching:
Yājnavalkya's long dialogue with King Janaka, or his shorter one with
his wife (*Brihadāranyaka Upanishad*, IV, 3-4; II, 4) can help us to
understand the idea that Brahman is pure consciousness without an object,
while *Chāndogya Upanishad*, VI contrasts learning with wisdom, and goes
on to a series of illustrations of the idea of Brahman (though without
using that word). These Upanishads speak of Brahman mainly as an impersonal being, the source of the universe and of consciousness, and the
highest object of knowledge; they may be contrasted with others such as
the short *Ishā Upanishad*, which speaks of a personal God, and the *Katha
Upanishad*, which suggests that salvation comes to those whom God chooses.
The first half of the *Katha Upanishad*, with its story of a wise brahmin
boy's confrontation with Death, and its analysis of a personality on the
analogy of a chariot, is a fruitful basis for discussion.
For translations of the Upanishads see Zaehner, *Hindu Scriptures*;
Hume, *Thirteen Principal Upanishads*; Parrinder, *The Wisdom of the Forest*.

2.5.2. *Post-Vedic Sanskrit literature*

Less ancient than the Veda are a large group of texts which Hindus traditionally call smriti 'memory, what is remembered'; unlike the Veda,
which is eternal, they are supposed to have been remembered by men from
the words of gods and sages. They include the epics, the law-books and
the Purānas.
The epics are the *Mahābhārata* and the *Rāmāyana*, composed in stages
between about 500 B.C. and 300 A.D. The first is about the five Pāndava

brothers and their dynastic struggle against their cousins, in which they
are aided by their ally Krishna, but contains digressions on many subjects; the second is about the prince Rāma, his exile and his fight with
the demon king Rāvana, and is the more approachable and easier to understand of the two epics. Both Krishna and Rāma are incarnations of
Vishnu. There are abridged translations of both by Dutt (in old-
fashioned verse), by Rajagopalachari, and by Raghavan (*The Indian
Heritage*), and one of the *Mahābhārata* by Narasimhan; also retellings
(Picard, *The Story of the Pandavas* and *The Story of Rama and Sita*;
Seeger, *The Five Sons of King Pandu*).

The best-known of the many digressions in the *Mahābhārata* is the
Bhagavadgītā. The Gītā is one of the world's greatest religious poems,
giving a vivid picture of God's power and love; it is a dialogue in which
Krishna, who is God, teaches his friend Arjuna. Parts of it may be
selected to illustrate particular topics, e.g.: II, 11-30 on the contrast
between samsāra and eternity; III, 4-35 on man's duty to the world; IV,
1-9 on avatārs; VI on yoga; VII on God as lord and saviour; IX, 20-34 on
lower and higher religion; XVI on the selfishness of the ungodly; XVIII,
41-8 on the duties of the four varnas; XVIII, 57-66 on the devotee's
total reliance on God. Chapter XI deserves a special place for the dra-
matic way in which it presents an awe-inspiring and terrifying vision of
God, seen mainly through the eyes of Arjuna. Edgerton (*The Bhagavadgītā*)
is the most accurate translation, but difficult for some; Zaehner has
published one with commentary (*The Bhagavadgītā*) and one without (*Hindu
Scriptures*).

There are several Sanskrit law-books (dharma-shāstra); the best-known
is *The Laws of Manu*, compiled in about the second century A.D. It begins
with a chapter which describes the origin of the world. These law-books
cover not only the law enforced by judges in courts, but all aspects of
dharma, including social relations, family organization and ritual.

The *Purānas* are a mass of texts on mythology and religion, mainly from
the fifth to eleventh centuries A.D. As a whole they are too difficult
for schools, but the selections in O'Flaherty, *Hindu Myths* are possible
in the sixth form, and so are the abridged translations in Raghavan,
The Indian Heritage. See also Archer, *The Loves of Krishna*, and 2.3.2.

The epics and Purānas contain many of the myths which are familiar to
Hindus today. Some of these myths are retold in the books listed in
2.3.4, p. 71.

2.5.3. *Vernacular literature*

Most Hindus learn Hinduism through the traditional literature in their
regional languages, mainly in verse. Many of the longer vernacular poems
are retellings of stories from the *Mahābhārata*, *Rāmāyana* and Purānas.
There are also many devotional poems, composed by poets who are often
revered as saints; they show how everyone can approach God, not only the
few high-caste people who know Sanskrit. The earliest poems of this
kind were composed in the Tamil language in South India in the seventh
century A.D.; from that time, the practice of writing such poems spread
northwards as part of what is known as the bhakti movement.

Ramanujan, *Speaking of Śiva* is a selection of the poetry of the
Lingāyat sect, translated from the Kannada language spoken in Karnātaka
(Mysore). Dimock and Levertov, *In Praise of Krishna*, is a selection of
Bengali poems on the love of the cowherd girls for Krishna, which

symbolizes the love of the worshipper for God. Archer, *The Loves of Krishna*, gives useful background.

2.5.4. *Secular literature*

Since religion and everyday life form one continuum in Hinduism, much can be learnt about it from texts that are not obviously religious. The art of story-telling is one at which Indians have excelled for centuries. The best-known collection of tales is the *Panchatantra*, written in several Sanskrit versions during the first millennium A.D. (translations by Ryder and by Edgerton; selection by Clark). Despite its use of animal characters, it was not written for children. It has a complex structure in which a character in one tale tells another tale, and so on, which makes the first tale difficult to follow. This complexity, together with the cynicism, cruelty or bawdiness of some of the tales, makes parts of it unsuitable for young children; but it deserves to be widely known, and its stories of lazy brahmins and fraudulent holy men show an outlook that is as authentically Hindu as that of more pious texts. Another ancient collection is the *Jātakas*, which were compiled by Buddhists from traditional sources (selection by Khan). See also Lefever, *One Man and His Dog*; Siek, *Favourite Tales from India*; Thapar, *Indian Tales*.

Modern fiction is valuable both for insight into ways of thinking and for details of everyday life. Banerji's *Pather Panchali* is an episodic, semi-autobiographical novel of brahmin life in rural Bengal. Rabīndranāth Tagore's novels are of more sophisticated Bengali life. His plays are set in the legendary past, and often show an enlightened person confronting the tyranny of conventional religion. His *The Golden Boat* is a collection of very short, evocative stories. Ananta Murthy's *Samskara* is a subtle short novel of a brahmin's unorthodox search for himself in the midst of a decaying traditional dharma. R.K. Narayan's novels are entertaining as well as giving a vivid picture of South Indian life. Some of Anita Desai's stories may be useful, especially *Village by the Sea*.

2.6. *THE HISTORICAL BACKGROUND OF HINDUISM*

2.6.0. *Introduction*

Since the term 'Hinduism' does not refer to a single creed, code of practice, or organization, it would be difficult to give a history of Hinduism. We cannot—as we can with Islam or Christianity, for instance—point to a date and say that as far as history is concerned that is where Hinduism begins. Nor can we separate the events that shaped Hinduism from the events of India's cultural, social and political history. The history of India and the history of Hinduism form one continuous whole.

India (using the term in the wider sense, to refer to the Indian subcontinent) is a land-mass measuring up to 2,000 miles from east to west and from north to south, containing about 700,000,000 people. It is bounded by sea to the south and by mountains to the north, and can be divided into two roughly equal areas. The first, peninsular India, is a triangle bounded on the south-west by the Arabian Sea and on the southeast by the Bay of Bengal, both of which are parts of the Indian Ocean. The second, northern India, is a quadrilateral bounded on the north by the great range of the Himalayas, 1,500 miles long and 10,000 feet high, and on the west and east by lesser but still formidable ranges. The mountains marking the division between these two main areas have repeatedly checked the southward expansion of northern empires.

Peninsular India is mountainous in the middle and has its main centres of population and political power along the coasts; northern India, more favourable to the growth of empires, is mountainous at the edges and has its centres along the Ganges and its tributaries, and to a lesser degree along the Indus.

India's natural external boundaries have given it a cultural unity which can be observed in many features found throughout the subcontinent, despite the great variety of Indian culture: in dress, a tendency to rely on large strips of cloth wrapped round the body, though sewn garments are also known; in food, a love of sweets and spices and a habit of eating with the fingers; in languages, a way of pronouncing certain *t* and *d* sounds with the tip of the tongue curled upwards; in society, the phenomena of caste and the joint family (2.2); in religious practice, the worship of images with gifts of food and clothing (2.1.1), and a reverence for holy men, living or dead; and in belief, the idea of a succession of births and deaths from which man can escape into an eternal state of perfection (2.4.1).

The external boundaries do not, however, seal off India from the outside world. Overland from the north-west have come Aryans, Greeks, Scythians, Huns, and a series of Muslim invaders; the western coast has been approached since the first century A.D. by Greek and later by Arab sailors, later still by the Portuguese and then by the British. The western coast has also provided homes for small communities of Christians, Jews and Parsis (Zoroastrians from Persia). Islam was brought to India, both by merchants and by invaders, soon after the time of Muhammad. Britain has been closely involved with the history of India since the mid-eighteenth century.

India, in turn, has influenced the outside world: Buddhism has spread to Central Asia, China, and South-east Asia, while the story of Rāma has been told and acted in many parts of South-east Asia for centuries.

Modern transport and communications bring people, foodstuffs, art, music and ideas to and fro between India and all parts of the world.

The whole of India has never been one political unit, though many ancient kings had the ambition of conquering all the land 'from the Himalayas to the ocean'. The British Indian empire, which came nearer to achieving this ambition than any other, ended with the partition of India in 1947. Within India are hundreds of peoples and tribes, speaking hundreds of languages, and following different ways of life in surroundings as varied as snow, tropical rain forest, and desert.

There are two main families of languages in India: Indo-Aryan and Dravidian. The Indo-Aryan family covers northern India and the northern part of peninsular India; it is a part of the Indo-European language family (which includes nearly every language in Europe, and also Persian). The most commonly spoken Indo-Aryan language is Hindi, which is spoken over a large part of northern India, and is the national language of the Republic of India. Sanskrit, the ancient literary language, is an Indo-Aryan language. Urdu, the national language of Pakistan, is also an Indo-Aryan language, but it uses a large number of Persian, Arabic and Turkish words. The Dravidian languages are spoken in the southern part of peninsular India; they are quite separate from the Indo-Aryan languages in origin, though through centuries of contact they have adopted many Indo-Aryan words. Tamil, one of the Dravidian languages, has a literature going back at least to the first century A.D. Some of the less widely used languages of India belong to neither of these families, while English is widely spoken as a second language.

Nearly three quarters of the Indian population are Hindus; nearly a quarter are Muslims, and there are smaller minorities of Sikhs, Buddhists, Jains, Parsis, Christians and Jews, as well as followers of tribal religions.

What follows is not a history but a series of sketches of some of the constituents which have made up Indian culture and affected the development of Hinduism.

2.6.1. *Pre-Aryan India*

Aryan influence, represented by Sanskrit, the authority of the Veda, and respect for brahmins, has gradually spread cver India from the north-west since about 1500 B.C. Before the coming of this influence there were pre-Aryan civilizations which have also left their mark on Indian culture and on Hinduism. Since the oldest known Indian literature is that of the Aryans, all we can know of pre-Aryan India (that is, India before about 1500 B.C.) comes from archaeology.

Stone implements have been found in India dating from as far back as 300,000 B.C., but the most exciting archaeological discovery has been that of the Harappan or Indus Valley Civilization, which flourished between 2500 and 1500 B.C. This civilization built cities of brick, with straight streets and elaborate provision for water supply, baths and drainage; it had a uniform system of weights and measures, and traded with the cities of Mesopotamia. It was first identified by archaeologists at Harappā in the Indus Valley in 1922, and is now known to have extended over a large part of north-west India. Its most tantalising legacy to the archaeologist is a great number of seals bearing writing in a strange script; many attempts have been made to read it, but none has proved convincing. Several of those who have tried to read

The Indian Subcontinent.

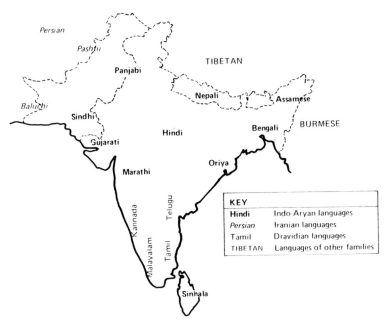

Languages of the Subcontinent.

the writing say it is a Dravidian language; since Dravidian languages still exist in isolated areas of northern India and were probably more widespread in earlier times, this is likely but not certain.

Much of what we now know as Hinduism may go back to the Harappan civilization. The worship of mother-goddesses seems to be a feature of pre-Aryan religion, since it contrasts markedly with the Aryan emphasis on male gods in religion and on the male line in family organization, and prevails especially in the south and east of India—the regions most remote from Aryan influence; it can be traced in the fertile-looking female figures found in the Harappan sites. Bathing, which is so important in Hinduism, was already well provided for in the Harappan cities. One of the Harappan seals is sometimes thought to show a proto-type of the god Shiva. It has even been held that the idea of rebirth (2.4.1) goes back to the Harappan civilization, though there is no positive evidence for this.

The discovery of the Harappan civilization has stimulated interest in pre-Aryan India, and shown that Indian history does not begin with the coming of the Aryans. However, much remains unknown, not only about the Harappans but about other civilizations which may have existed.

2.6.1.1. *Resources*

Bahree, *India, Pakistan and Bangladesh*, 9-21.
Basham (ed.), *A Cultural History of India*, 11-19.
Basham, *The Wonder That Was India*, 10-28.
Nehru, *The Discovery of India*, ch. IV.

2.6.2. *The Aryans and the Veda*

Some time around 1500 B.C., a distinct group of people entered north-west India. They must have entered from what is now Afghanistan, though where they came from before that is uncertain. Their language was an Indo-European one, closely related to the Iranian languages (of which Persian is the main modern representative) but distinct from them.

They called themselves Ārya; this name has been anglicized as 'Aryan' (see Glossary under *Aryan*). They despised the non-Aryan peoples, and treated them either as enemies or as slaves. They did not come as a single invading force, but in a number of groups over a long period; they fought against each other as well as against the non-Aryan peoples. They probably did not come in great numbers, but they overpowered the non-Aryans with a means of warfare hitherto unknown in India: the horse-drawn chariot. Whether it was the Aryans who destroyed the Harappan civilization, or whether the Harappan civilization perished before the Aryans appeared, is uncertain.

Unlike the Harappans, the Aryans had no writing system; but they had a literature, composed in an early form of Sanskrit, which they handed down orally from teacher to pupil, and recited as part of their ritual. This they called the Veda, meaning 'knowledge' (2.5.1), and it is from it that modern scholars have derived most of what is known of these early Aryans, the Vedic Aryans as they are called. Their religion was very different from Hinduism: there were no images or temples, and in the earliest parts of the Veda there was no idea of rebirth. Rudra (later called Shiva) and Vishnu were worshipped, but they are not men-tioned nearly so often in the Veda as some other gods who have since lapsed into relative obscurity—notably the warrior god Indra (2.3.1). In the later parts of the Veda—the Upanishads, composed from about 600 B.C. onwards—rebirth is known, and so is the idea that knowledge of Brahman is man's highest possible achievement. These ideas have sur-vived as among the most distinctive in Hinduism.

The Vedic Aryans left other important legacies to Hinduism. They had brought with them into India a social theory which divided society into three functional groups: the priesthood, the warrior nobility, and the people. When they subdued the non-Aryan people, they added these as a fourth group, thus forming the Hindu theory of the four varnas, in which the first three varnas are Aryan or Twice-born, while the fourth, whose duty is to serve the others, is non-Aryan (2.2.2). An important part of this theory is the position of the brahmins, who perform the worship of the gods on behalf of others, especially wealthy kings, and in Vedic times were rewarded with gifts of cattle. In Hinduism today, the relationship between a brahmin and those for whom he performs ritual is modelled on the relationship between the Vedic brahmins and kings. The brahmin who performs rituals for a Hindu family (2.2.1) is called the purohita, which is the Vedic term for a king's chief priest; and a cow is still one of the traditional forms of gift to a brahmin, though it is usually represented by a coin.

In order to preserve the Veda in the absence of writing, it was necessary for some Aryan boys to undergo a lengthy and rigorous training in which they learnt the texts by heart. This practice survives in the thread-ceremony, the rite in which a boy is placed in the charge of a brahmin (2.1.2). Though the old Vedic ritual is rarely performed, certain Vedic verses or mantras are widely known, particularly the

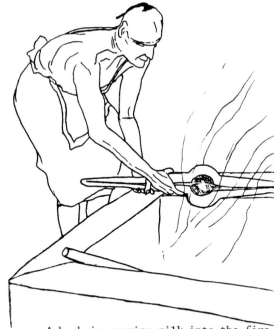

A brahmin pouring milk into the fire
at a Vedic sacrifice.

Gāyatrī (2.1.1; 2.1.2; 2.5.1). The Sanskrit language has been cultivated by learned Hindus, as well as by Jains, Buddhists and some non-
Hindus, down to the present day; it has contributed words to the
vocabulary of all the Indian literary languages. The brahmins, who
already in early Vedic times were royal advisers as well as priests,
have maintained a position of leadership: under Hindu, Muslim and
British rulers they filled a large number of official positions, and in
the present Republic of India the number of brahmins in the professions
and in politics is greatly out of proportion to their number in the
population. Even among the Marxist intelligentsia, which opposes all
traditional forms of authority, many prominent thinkers are brahmins.
All these features of Indian life are legacies of the Vedic Aryans.
  During Vedic times, Aryan influence spread from north-west India into
the Ganges basin. Later it spread further eastwards and southwards, so
that by the first century A.D. Aryan ideas had spread to the extreme
south of India. This spread of Aryan ideas does not mean that the
Aryans migrated in large numbers and expelled or subjugated the non-
Aryan people; rather, the prestige of Sanskrit learning, and belief in
the power of the rituals performed by brahmins and in the value of the
Aryan way of life, were accepted over an increasing area. People
adopted the norms laid down in the Sanskrit shāstras, and kings were
eager to have brahmins at their courts. This process is sometimes
called Aryanization or Sanskritization; it occurred in South-east Asia
as well as in India.
  The Aryan population soon merged and intermarried with the non-Aryan.

Though for ritual purposes some castes are Aryan and others not, this
does not mean that they are descended exclusively from the Vedic Aryans
and the pre-Aryan peoples respectively. All Indians, like other peoples,
are of mixed ancestry, and the difference between Aryan and non-Aryan
is mainly a matter of culture and of ritual status, not of descent.

2.6.2.1. *Resources*

Bahree, *India, Pakistan and Bangladesh*, 22-6.
Basham (ed.), *A Cultural History of India*, 20-9.
Basham, *The Wonder That Was India*, 28-43; 232-56.
Nehru, *The Discovery of India*, ch. IV.
Thapar and Spear, *A History of India*, I, 28-49.

2.6.3. *Kings and cities*

The Aryans who entered north-west India were a people on the move, in
search of new pastures for their cattle; they built neither cities nor
temples, unlike the Harappan people, who certainly had cities though
none of their buildings have been certainly identified as temples. Their
kings ruled over tribes rather than territories, and their priests
worshipped the gods on ground sanctified for the occasion, not at permanent holy places. But as the Aryan culture became integrated with the
non-Aryan, it became city-based: wealth was counted in gold rather than
cattle, and the merchant took over economic leadership from the herdsman,
a change which can be traced back to the time of the early Upanishads
around the sixth century B.C. Probably as part of the same process, the
mobile Vedic cult gave way to temple worship. Among the non-Aryans,
there had probably always been simple open-air worship at sacred rocks
and trees, of the kind that exists in India today; the Hindu temple is
an elaboration of this kind of permanent sacred place. By identifying
the local god with one of the Aryan gods, by using Sanskrit texts in the
worship of the local god, and by appointing brahmin priests to minister
to him, the local cult becomes Aryanized.

Though some writers treat the Vedic religion as a form of Hinduism,
it is customary to draw a distinction between the two; the main difference is, as suggested here, that Hinduism has temples and other sacred
places while the Vedic religion does not. The distinction is not a
hard and fast one, however, since elements of Vedic religion still survive in Hinduism.

As the city became the centre of economic and political power, it also
became important in the history of religion. Kings rewarded brahmins
with grants of land, which enabled the brahmins to live on their rents;
wealthy merchants also gave them money. Land and money were granted to
temples in the same way, so that a temple could become a wealthy land-
owner employing a large staff. Other kings, such as Ashoka in the third
century B.C. (2.7.2), patronized Buddhist monasteries, and others
patronized Jain monasteries, so that the fortunes of Buddhism, Jainism
and the various Hindu sects rose and fell as the kings who supported
each religion rose and fell or were converted from one religion to
another.

Royal patronage assisted the rise and spread of bhakti (devotion to
God). Already in the *Bhagavadgītā* (perhaps about 200 B.C.) we find
God—in the form of Krishna—promising his devotees that he will return

their love and bring them to salvation; but what is usually called the 'bhakti movement' begins in the seventh century A.D. in South India, where Tamil saints expressed their love of God in poetry, some seeing him as Vishnu and some as Shiva. These saint-poets, and the Hindu kings who listened to them, helped Hinduism to overcome Buddhism and Jainism in South India. During the next few centuries the movement spread northwards, inspiring poetry in the vernacular languages of India and so helping to fuse popular religion with the Sanskrit tradition.

The kings also encouraged Sanskrit learning: court poets sang their praises in Sanskrit, and wrote Sanskrit plays and poems to entertain them; they employed brahmin advisers and pandits and collected libraries. The status enjoyed by learned men encouraged the production of philosophical and theological writing, and ideas were constantly refined and sharpened through argument, both between different Hindu sects and between Hindus and Buddhists or other opponents of Vedic and brahmin authority. Sometimes kings arranged and presided over public debates between rival thinkers, a practice which has continued into modern times.

It was the ambition of ancient Indian kings to conquer the world; in practice, power was shared among many rival dynasties based on different cities. Sometimes one dynasty built an empire by overcoming others, such as the Mauryan empire inherited by Ashoka (2.7.2), or the Gupta empire in the fourth to sixth centuries A.D. Many dynasties ruled only small areas, and frontiers were always fluid.

Hindu kingdoms, especially in peninsular India, continued into the Muslim period and acted as a check to the spread of Muslim rule. The last great Hindu empire, that of the Marāthās (2.7.8), controlled large parts of western peninsular India in the seventeenth and eighteenth centuries, and was only finally overthrown by the British in 1818. Many kingdoms continued to exist in the British period as 'princely states', having a measure of internal autonomy but bound to the British by treaties (2.6.5). Their rājās (kings) and mahārājās (great kings), some ruling large states like Kashmir or Mysore, others only a few square miles, were not always playboys; some were conscientious rulers, continuing their traditional patronage to temples and learned brahmins.

2.6.3.1. *Resources*

Bahree, *India, Pakistan and Bangladesh*, 26-40.
Basham (ed.), *A Cultural History of India*, 38-59.
Basham, *The Wonder That Was India*, 44-231; 256-346.
Nehru, *The Discovery of India*, ch. IV-V.
Thapar and Spear, *A History of India*, I, 70-265.

2.6.4. *Muslim rule*

India has long been open to penetration from the west, both by land from Iran and by sea from Arabia. It is natural, therefore, that the expansion of Islam in the seventh century A.D. soon reached western India. Sind (the country round the lower part of the Indus) was conquered by Arabs in the early eighth century. Early in the eleventh century Sultān Mahmūd of Ghaznī, in what is now Afghanistan, overran the Panjab and reached as far as Gujarat in north-western peninsular India, where he sacked the great temple at Somnāthpur. A Muslim sultanate was established at Delhi in 1206, and continued, under a series of dynasties of Turkish and Afghan origin, into the early

sixteenth century; the position of Delhi as the capital of India is a
legacy of this period. The areas controlled by the Delhi Sultanate
varied; at times it controlled most of northern India and even most of
the peninsula as well, but at other times it was reduced to Delhi and
its surroundings.

The last and most successful of the Muslim dynasties, the Mughals,
established a new empire on the ruins of the old Delhi Sultanate. The
Mughals were descendants of the great Turkish conqueror Tīmūr or
Tamerlane (d. 1405), who was of part-Mongol blood. Their title was not
Sultān but Pādshāh (Persian for 'emperor'), and they ruled in Delhi con-
tinuously from 1555 until the last Mughal emperor was deposed by the
British in 1858. At the height of their power, at the beginning of the
eighteenth century, they controlled all but the far south of India.

The period of Muslim rule in India was not simply one of domination of
Hindus by Muslims. Many Hindu powers flourished, especially in peninsular India which is protected from the north by mountains; the greatest
of these powers was based on the city of Vijayanagar. Moreover, the
Delhi rulers often had to contend with rival Muslim powers established
in other parts of India. In fact, the old struggle between rival kingdoms to extend their power continued, with the difference that now some
of the rivals were Hindu and others Muslim.

The establishment of Muslim power led to the conversion of many Hindus
to Islam; conversion, rather than immigration, accounts for the fact
that nearly a quarter of today's Indian population are Muslim. On the
other hand Islam was not forced on the Indian population as a whole.
Many Muslim rulers, adapting themselves to Indian notions of the function
of a king, carried on the custom of patronage to brahmins and temples.
The Mughal emperor Akbar (reigned 1560-1605) carried tolerance so far
as to invite not only Muslim teachers but Hindu pandits, Parsis, Jains
and even Jesuits to discuss religion at his court; on the other hand
his great-grandson Aurangzeb (reigned 1658-1707) insisted on maintaining the purity of Islam.

The Muslim dynasties brought to India a Muslim culture which owed much
to Iran. Persian was the court language at first, and was later joined
by Urdu, a language resembling Hindi but using Persian, Arabic and
Turkish words. Like the Aryans and other invaders before them, the
Muslims became integrated into Indian society. Hindus served in the
army and civil service under Muslim rulers, while Muslims took service
under Hindus. Hindus who lived in cities where Islamic culture
flourished would enjoy and compose Persian and Urdu literature, while
many Muslims took an interest in Sanskrit and Hindi. The domes, arches
and minarets of Islamic architecture graced Indian cities, and Hindu
myths were illustrated in styles influenced by Persian painting. Under
the Mughals the culture of the court became even more cosmopolitan, as
European commercial and political interest in India increased.

Hindu and Muslim cultures interpenetrated in the sphere of religion
also. The Sūfīs—Muslim mystics—found kindred spirits among the
Hindus, while some Hindus were attracted to Muslim ideas of the equality
of man and the worship of one formless God. While the formal tradition
of Sanskrit learning largely ignored the existence of Islam, the popular
bhakti movement was well aware of the presence of two thoroughly different religions in India. Kabīr (1440-1518), one of the great poets of
the bhakti tradition, held that the differences between Hinduism and
Islam in doctrine and practice had no meaning for a real devotee; God

was the same in temple and mosque, and the only true worship was in the heart, not in words or actions. Nānak (2.7.4) preached a similar message; his followers, the Sikhs, formed a new religion which was neither Muslim nor Hindu.

The effects of Muslim culture on India can be seen today, among Hindus as well as Muslims, especially in northern India. Persian and Arabic words are used in everyday speech. Hindus venerate the tombs of Muslim saints, while Muslims sometimes go to Hindu holy men for advice. Hindus and Muslims can enjoy the same Indian poetry, music and even food. But there has also been strife and distrust, which led eventually to the partition of India and the massacres which accompanied it.

2.6.4.1. *Resources*

Bahree, *India, Pakistan and Bangladesh*, 41-58.
Basham (ed.), *A Cultural History of India*, 245-333.
Nehru, *The Discovery of India*, ch. VI.
Thapar and Spear, *A History of India*, I, 266-336; II, 15-80.

2.6.5. *British rule*

During the Mughal period, India became involved in the search by Western European countries for new lands with which to trade. Britain, Denmark, France, the Netherlands and Portugal all established trading posts in India; but the British, following Robert Clive's successful struggle with the French for supremacy in India in the mid-eighteenth century, had the most far-reaching effect on Indian history.

The East India Company had been founded in 1600. By the eighteenth century it had three main trading posts, or presidencies as they were called, at Bombay, Calcutta and Madras. In order to secure its trading position, the Company raised its own armies, interfered in struggles between Indian powers, and from 1757 onwards began to control territories, nominally as an agent of the Mughal emperor but in effect as an increasingly independent power. In this way it changed from a trading company to a unique political and military organization, maintaining itself from revenue collected in its territories, while the Mughal emperor in Delhi became a mere puppet and pensioner of the Company.

At first the Company was answerable only to its own Court of Directors in London, but in a series of Acts of Parliament from 1773 onwards it was gradually brought under the control of the British Government; finally, in 1858, the Company was dissolved and its powers transferred to the Crown.

During the same period the Company annexed increasing areas of India, while in other areas it concluded treaties with Indian rulers which obliged them to accept the advice of British officials, known as 'residents' or (where several small states were grouped together) 'political agents'. Such areas were called 'princely states', 'native states', or simply 'states'. By the end of the nineteenth century the British had come to rule the whole of India, directly or indirectly, except for a few small colonies retained by France and Portugal (the Himalayan states of Nepal, Sikkim and Bhutan were also wholly or partly under British control, as were neighbouring Afghanistan, Burma and Ceylon (now Sri Lanka)).

The centres of British influence and expansion were the three 'presidency towns' of Bombay, Calcutta and Madras. Calcutta was the

foremost of the three; it was the capital of British India and the seat
of the Governor-General of India (known also, from 1858, as the Viceroy).
In 1912, however, the capital was moved to the old Mughal capital, Delhi.

The British were far from being the first rulers of foreign origin in
India; but they were the first to establish an extensive Indian empire
while retaining a base outside India to which they were responsible and
to which they expected to return when they retired. They were not absorbed into Indian life as former ruling peoples had been; on the contrary, with improvements in communications in the nineteenth and twentieth centuries they became less Indianized and more in touch with
Britain than they had been in the eighteenth century.

Yet, perhaps for this very reason, the effect of the British presence
in India has been profound. It introduced a new all-India language,
English, more widely known in India today than Sanskrit, Persian or
Urdu had ever been; at the same time, through printing and other forms
of communication, it encouraged the growth of literature in the regional
vernacular languages. Education was promoted by Government, missionaries
and independent societies, in which Indians took a leading part; universities were set up in Bombay, Calcutta and Madras in 1856, and others
followed. New opportunities in commerce, the professions and government
service led to the growth of a new English-speaking urban middle class.

The new urban middle class, cut off from traditional forms of teaching,
felt a desire to find roots in the Hindu tradition, and this desire was
met by new ways of presenting Hinduism: organizations like the Brāhmo Samāj
and Ārya Samāj, which used some of the methods of Christian churches;
books and lectures, often in English; and Hindu educational and cultural
organizations. Through translations and printing, some of the ancient
Sanskrit texts of Hinduism became more widely known, especially the
Upanishads and the *Bhagavadgītā*; in the twentieth century, lectures and
classes on the *Bhagavadgītā* became ways of disseminating Hindu ideas,
alongside the more exclusive traditional ways.

Besides opening up new lines of communication both within and outside
India, the British did many things which were offensive to Hindus.
Nineteenth-century legislation which interfered with Hindu customs
aroused opposition; despite official reluctance to interfere in religion,
it was suspected that Christian missionaries were receiving government
backing in an attempt to destroy Hinduism. The mutiny of 1857, which
took place among both Hindu and Muslim soldiers in the Company's army,
and was supported by several Indian rulers, was a protest against
interference with traditional customs.

Moreover, the new middle class, encouraged by European ideas of
liberty, democracy and nationhood, and frustrated by unfulfilled official
promises of participation in government, became in the late nineteenth
century outspokenly critical of the British. In the 1890s, political
demands and religious grievances met together to form a new religious
nationalism, which regarded 'Mother India' (a new concept) as a form of
the Goddess who needed to be rescued by her devotees from foreign
oppression; the freedom of the nation became a goal almost as desirable
as moksha (salvation, man's freedom from the world) itself. The eternal
dharma was seen to be in danger, and it was the duty of Hindus to preserve it and eventually to teach it to the whole world.

When nationalism rallied round Hinduism in this way, it tended to ex-
clude or even antagonize Muslims, who turned to the British for protection against Hindu communal feeling. For a time, during the First World

War and in the 1920s, Hindu and Muslim politicians tried to work
together in the freedom movement, encouraged by people like Tagore,
Gāndhī and Rādhākrishnan, to whom true religion was above distinctions
of creed or community. While these proclaimed that India was one nation,
many Muslims insisted that it was two nations, the Hindus and the Muslims,
and distrusted the Hindu-led movement. In the 1930s, this distrust found
expression in the demand for a separate Muslim country.

2.6.5.1. *Resources*

Bahree, *India, Pakistan and Bangladesh*, 59-67.
Basham (ed.), *A Cultural History of India*, 348-422.
De Bary (ed.), *Sources of Indian Tradition*, II.
Nehru, *The Discovery of India*, ch. VII-X.
Thapar and Spear, *A History of India*, II, 81-220.

2.6.6. *Independence*

Because of the tensions described above, which led to communal riots
and massacres, India achieved independence in 1947 not as one country
but as two: India and Pakistan (the latter name was coined in 1933).
Pakistan consisted of two wings, one in the Indus region and the other
in East Bengal, separated by a thousand miles of Indian territory; in
1971, the eastern wing separated to become Bangladesh. The remainder
of the subcontinent (excluding Bhutan, Nepal, Sikkim and Sri Lanka)
became what is now known as India; when referring to the whole subcontinent after 1947, therefore, we have to speak of 'the subcontinent'
or (if we wish to include Sri Lanka and other neighbouring countries)
'South Asia'.
   Partition was designed to separate those parts of India which had a
Muslim majority from those with a Hindu majority. Nevertheless the new
India still had about a 10% minority of Muslims, and Pakistan had about
a 10% minority of Hindus; since the latter were mainly in East Pakistan,
now Bangladesh, the Hindu population of present-day Pakistan is much
smaller. Over seven million people fled from each of the two new
countries to the other, while thousands died from privation and violence.
   In each country, the princely states were dismantled and absorbed into
the new political structure, ending an institution which can be traced
back to Vedic times.
   While Pakistan is an Islamic state, the Republic of India is not a
Hindu state but a secular state; its Constitution takes a neutral attitude to all religions, and its Sanskrit motto, satyam eva jayate 'Truth
alone conquers', taken from the *Mahābhārata*, does not imply that truth
belongs to any particular creed. The Constitution proclaims the equality
of all citizens irrespective of religion, race, caste, sex and place of
birth, and expressly outlaws untouchability. Nevertheless, Indian
legislation has had to recognize caste, in order to provide positive
discrimination in favour of the Untouchables in education and employment.
   India and Bangladesh are members of the Commonwealth; Pakistan left
the Commonwealth in 1972. English continues to be used in all three
countries, together with vernacular languages, in government, higher
education, business and literature, giving the subcontinent a special
relationship with the rest of the English-speaking world. Hinduism is
studied in about a dozen British universities and many schools, and
there is a growing body of books about it for Western readers.

2.6.6.1. *Resources*

Basham (ed.), *A Cultural History of India*, 487-99.
Thapar and Spear, *A History of India*, II, 221-56.

2.6.7. *Migration*

Indians have been travelling by sea to South-east Asia and East Africa,
and by land to many parts of Asia, for centuries. In the nineteenth and
early twentieth centuries, large numbers of Indians were recruited to
work in parts of the British empire where there was a demand for labour,
especially in plantations and on railways. The methods of recruitment
and the conditions of service were sometimes little better than kidnap-
ping and slavery, but were gradually brought under control by the
Government of India, which finally banned mass recruitment for work
overseas in 1938.

Employers in the same area overseas tended to recruit from the same
part of India, and since the men often went back to India after some
years, sometimes marrying and going overseas again with their wives,
firm links were formed between places of recruitment in India and places
of employment overseas. As well as labourers there were craftsmen,
clerks, shopkeepers and professional people who made their way to places
where their work was in demand; again, people from the same area in India
tended to go to the same area overseas, where they would fit into the
same network of caste, village and family relationships which they had
belonged to in India. In this way were formed the communities of Panjabi
and Gujarati railway workers, craftsmen and traders from western India
in East Africa, Tamil rubber estate workers from South India in Malaya,
Behari sugar-cane workers from the Ganges basin in the Caribbean, Sikh
policemen from north-western India in Hong Kong, and so on. These communities did their best to educate their children in their ancestral
languages as well as in the languages of their adopted countries, to
worship in their own temples, mosques or gurdwaras (Sikh temples), and
to carry on their Indian traditions. It has been estimated that there
are about five million people of Indian origin (including what would now
be Pakistani or Bangladeshi origin) outside India.

Because of the special relationship between India and the United
Kingdom, which has been intimately connected with India since the
eighteenth century and assumed full responsibility for its government
from 1858 until 1947, Indians have been coming to this country since
the nineteenth century as students, doctors, seamen, soldiers, traders,
and others. Though there were no large communities of Indians in
Britain until after Independence, many Indians worked in Britain, either
with their families or in groups of men living together cheaply and
working hard till they could save enough to return to India or bring
their families out.

The upheavals accompanying the partition of India in 1947 sent refu-
gees not only from the new Indian Union to Pakistan and vice versa, but
overseas as well. Many of these came to Britain. Another upheaval came
in the 1960s when Indians were forced out of Kenya, Uganda, Tanzania and
Zambia; many of these, too, came to Britain. However, immigration to
Britain has been increasingly restricted by the Commonwealth Immigration
Acts of 1962, 1968 and 1971. In Britain today there are about a million
people of Indian, Pakistani or Bangladeshi origin. They are often
referred to simply as 'Asians', though 'South Asians' is a more precise

term. About three hundred thousand of them are Hindus, mainly from Gujarat, the second largest group being from Panjab.

The main concentrations of Hindus in Britain are in London, Birmingham, Manchester, Leeds, Bradford, Leicester, Coventry and Nottingham; there are groups in many other industrial cities. Members of different Hindu communities predominate in different British cities: Gujarati followers of Swāminārāyan in north-west London, other Gujaratis in Coventry, Leicester and other cities, Panjabis in Newcastle upon Tyne, and so on. Hindus from many other parts of India are to be found all over Britain, especially in the professions.

Hindus (and Indians of other religions) in Britain retain their religious and social system, with modifications to suit new circumstances. Many keep up links with relatives in India, and marry brides from their ancestral region. Food rules cannot be kept as rigidly as in India, and patterns of worship are modified for several reasons. The British working week tends to restrict religious activities to Saturdays and Sundays, and it may not be possible to take time off for festivals; for similar reasons, the timing of rituals tends to go by the clock rather than by the sun. There is a shortage of the kind of people who hand on religious traditions in an Indian village: family elders, temple priests, purohitas, story-tellers and so on. An increasing proportion of Hindus in Britain are not immigrants but British-born, and share the speech, educational and working background, tastes and habits of other British people of the same locality. To retain their ancestral language, culture and religion costs them and their parents a special effort.

The temple has taken on new roles; it can be a cultural centre, a place where traditional food is prepared and eaten, a place where language classes and classes in religious instruction are held. Where there is no temple, groups meet for worship and cultural activities in private houses, but they often hope to collect enough money to start a temple, often in a converted church or hall. A further ambition is to have an image brought from India, installed by a brahmin with the proper ceremony, and worshipped daily thereafter; but this is harder to achieve. Brahmins are relatively few among British Hindus, and those learned in texts and ritual are even fewer. Necessity leads to modifications in ritual; non-brahmins or women often take roles which in India would be taken by a brahmin man.

Since 1970 there has been a great increase in the number of Hindu temples in Britain; there are now over a hundred. Krishna and Rāma are the deities most commonly worshipped, but there are temples of Shiva also. Sometimes friction arises from the need of the temple to cater for people of different Indian backgrounds; but often these difficulties are overcome by the tendency of Hinduism to recognize the validity of all forms and objects of worship. Where there are large numbers, as in London, there are several temples belonging to different groups.

Because pandits who specialize in performing rituals and reciting texts are hard to find, Hindus outside India often turn for religious leadership and teaching to relatively new organizations, such as the Ārya Samāj, the Rāmakrishna Mission, and the Swāminārāyan Hindu Mission, all of which originated in the nineteenth century. Others follow contemporary gurus such as Satya Sai Bābā (1926-).

Whether the Hindus and other people of Indian origin in Britain can take a respected and secure place in British society depends not only on how they adapt to British life, but also on how well other people in Britain understand their need to maintain their ancestral ways and traditions.

2.6.7.1. *Resources*

Bowen, *Hinduism in England*.
Bridger, *A Hindu Family in Britain*.
Ewan, *Understanding Your Hindu Neighbour*.
Harrison, *Hinduism in Preston*.
Kanitkar and Jackson, *Hindus in Britain*.
Taylor, *The Half-way Generation*.

BBC audio-cassette, *A Hindu Community in Britain*.

2.7. GREAT PEOPLE OF THE HINDU WORLD

2.7.0. *Introduction*

The study of outstanding people is a useful way of introducing a culture; by seeing what kind of people are remembered, and what they are remembered for, we can gain an insight into the culture's system of values.

The title 'Great people of the Hindu world' has been chosen, rather than 'Great Hindus', because many of the people who may usefully come into a study of Hinduism were not Hindus in a strict sense. The Buddha rejected the Veda and founded a new religion; Nehru was a humanist. Rammohun Roy was rejected by orthodox Hindus, though he wore the sacred thread till his death; Gāndhī was assassinated by a Hindu extremist who considered him an enemy of Hinduism. But they are undoubtedly products of Hindu thought and life, and many Hindus acknowledge their greatness in a typically Hindu way: by putting flowers on their images or pictures.

Seventeen examples are given below from among many possible subjects. They are selected to illustrate a variety of themes, and may be studied in different ways by different kinds of pupil. Young children may use the picture stories in the *Amar Chitra Kathā* series.

2.7.1. *The Buddha* (c. 560-480 B.C.): religious teacher.
Buddha is not a name, but a title meaning 'enlightened'. The prince Siddhārtha, of the Gautama family, ran away from his palace to seek release from the inevitable miseries of life: pain, old age, disease, death. Not satisfied with any current teachings, he found the truth by meditation, sitting under a tree known from that event as the Bodhi ('enlightenment') tree. From that time onwards he was the Buddha; thereafter he taught a band of disciples who became the first Buddhist monks. Hindus say he was an incarnation of Vishnu (2.3.1).

Amar Chitra Kathā, No. 22.
Basham, *The Wonder That Was India*, 256-61.

2.7.2. *Ashoka* (? - c. 232 B.C.): emperor.
In 269 B.C. he inherited the empire which had been built by his grandfather Chandragupta Maurya, with its capital at Pātaliputra (modern Patna); he extended it to cover all but the extreme east and south of India. His edicts are recorded in inscriptions, in which he claims that he has renounced wars of conquest, and intends to rule through righteousness (dharma). He became a Buddhist, banned animal sacrifices, and reduced the slaughter of animals for meat. He laid down regulations for Buddhist monks, and respected all other religions.

Amar Chitra Kathā, No. 37.
Basham, *The Wonder That Was India*, 53-7.

2.7.3. *Shankara* (? 788-820): philosopher, theologian and religious leader.
He was born in Kerala, South India, and tradition says that he took the sacred thread at the age of five, became a sannyāsī at eight, and wrote his greatest book at twelve. His teachings are called Advaita Vedānta (2.4.2) and are the most influential in Hinduism.

Shankara is said to have travelled all over India, not only defeating his opponents in argument but also organizing religious institutions.

Devotional hymns as well as learned works, all in Sanskrit, are attribu-
ted to him.

Amar Chitra Katha, No. 60.
Basham, *The Wonder That Was India*, 327-8.
Mahadevan, *Ten Saints of India*, 76-94.

2.7.4. *Nānak* (1469-1539): Panjabi teacher and poet, founder of the Sikhs,
who know him as Guru Nānak. Born a Hindu, he spent some years in wandering and learning from Hindu and Muslim teachers. He taught men to meditate on God by means of his Name, which is Truth itself, and to worship
him without images or ritual.

Amar Chitra Katha, No. 47.

2.7.5. *Chaitanya* (1485-1533): Bengali devotee of Krishna. He loved to
dance, sing and repeat the name of Krishna, seeing him and hearing his
flute everywhere. Often he was so rapt in ecstasy that people thought
him mad. Though he wrote nothing, he attracted many disciples; with
them, he founded the Vaishnava sect of Bengal, which regards Krishna as
the supreme form of God and makes much use of singing and dancing in its
worship. This sect has recently been brought to the West, under the
name of the International Society for Krishna Consciousness, commonly
known as the Hare Krishna movement.

Amar Chitra Katha, No. 90.
Sarma, *Hinduism Through the Ages*, 54-7.

2.7.6. *Rāna (King) Pratāp* (1540-1597): King of Mewar in Rajasthan, the
greatest of the fighting princes (Rājputs) for whom Rajasthan is famous.
While the other princes of Rajasthan, including his own brother, allied
themselves with the Mughal emperor Akbar, Pratāp resisted. For a time
he was defeated and took to the hills, but he continued the fight and
recovered some of his lost fortresses. He is remembered in the traditional heroic poetry of Rajasthan.

Amar Chitra Katha, No. 24.

2.7.7. *Mīrā Bāī* (? 1547-1614): a princess of Chitor in Rajasthan, who
became one of the great saint-poets of bhakti. She was so devoted to
Krishna that she thought of him as her lover and bridegroom. Married
to a prince at the age of eight, she continued singing her songs to
Krishna, and was persecuted by her husband's family, especially after
his early death. She became a pilgrim, and spent the last part of her
life in a temple of Krishna at Dwārakā, a holy city on the west coast.
Her poems are said to have so moved the god that he allowed her finally
to disappear into his idol in the temple—a miracle which consummated
her mystical marriage. Her poems express her constant devotion to
Krishna, whom she calls Giridhar 'lifter of the mountain', and refer to
her indifference to the hostility of the world, especially the relatives
of her earthly husband:

> My only consort is Giridhar Gopāl, none else—none else
> indeed in the whole world which I have seen through and through.
> I have forsaken my brother, friends, and relations, one and
> all, and sitting among saintly souls, have lost regard for

worldly fame or honour...The King sent me a cup of
poison, even that I have drunk with pleasure! The news is
now public, everyone now knows that Mīrā is deeply attached by
love to God; it does not matter now; what was fated has
happened!   (translator: V. Raghavan)

2.7.8. *Shivājī* (c. 1629-1680): a chieftain among the Marāthās, a warlike
people in the mountainous country of Mahārāshtra in Western India. He
fought successfully against Aurangzeb, the last great Mughal emperor, as
well as against lesser powers. Once, when imprisoned on a visit to
Aurangzeb at Āgrā, he and his son escaped by hiding in fruit baskets.
He made himself king in 1674, and left an empire which united the Marāthā
people, overtook the Mughal empire as the dominant power in India, and
remained until it was suppressed by the British in 1818. An annual
festival in his honour was started in 1896.

Shivājī was inspired by the Marāthī bhakti poets of his time, especially his guru Rāmdās, who wrote of the duty to protect brahmins,
the gods, the dharma and the cow. He respected other religions also;
he not only spared Portuguese Christian monks, mosques, and copies of
the Qur'ān in his campaigns, but venerated Muslim saints and gave
grants of land to mosques.

Amar Chitra Kathā, No. 23.
Thapar and Spear, *A History of India*, II, 58-60.

2.7.9. *Rāmmohun Roy* (? 1772-1833): Bengali brahmin, the first Indian to
write on religion in English. He translated Upanishads and other
Sanskrit texts into Bengali and English, and taught the worship of one
true God who is known in all religions. In 1828 he founded an organization, the Brahmo Samaj, for the worship of God as a formless being who
is beyond our comprehension but is known in our hearts. He wrote hymns
in Bengali, one of which runs:

> At home or abroad, wherever I may seek you,
> I see you in your creation, and I greet you.
> Your boundless creation constantly bears witness,
> At all times and places, to your greatness.
> I am not alone; I see your power and meet you.

Rammohun also wrote tracts against suttee, the practice of burning a
widow on her husband's funeral pyre. He sailed to England in 1830, and
died in Bristol in 1833.

Sarma, *Hinduism Through the Ages*, 60-4.

2.7.10. *Lakshmī Bāī* (1835-1858): Rānī (Queen) of Jhansī, a small state
in Central India. She was an outstanding leader in the Indian Mutiny
against the British in 1857-1858, and was killed as she rode in battle,
dressed as a man.

Amar Chitra Kathā, No. 51.

2.7.11. *Rāmakrishna* (1836-1886): Bengali saint. He knew little Sanskrit
and despised education; he learnt from wandering teachers and from his
own religious experience. His religious feelings were so intense that
he often went into trances or behaved in strange ways which made his

Rāmakrishna

family and friends think he was mad or ill. Though he was married, he
became a sannyāsī. His teachings were given in simple sayings and
stories; many influential people of his time came to listen to him. He
held that all religions were ways to the same truth, and believed that
he had reached that truth not only through Hinduism but through Islam
and Christianity. The Rāmakrishna Mission, a world-wide organization,
was founded after his death by Swāmī Vivekānanda.

Mahadevan, *Ten Saints of India*, 106-16.
Ramakrishna for Children.
Sarma, *Hinduism Through the Ages*, 117-38.
Tales from Ramakrishna.

2.7.12. *Swāmī Vivekānanda* (1862-1902): Bengali monk. A graduate of
Calcutta University, he had a completely different background from
Rāmakrishna; but Rāmakrishna taught him the value of the Hindu beliefs
which modern Indians such as he had been trying to forget, and the
limitations of the rationalistic outlook. Vivekānanda came to believe
that Advaita Vedānta (2.4.2) was the essence of Hinduism, and should
be taught to the whole world. He became a sannyāsī, and founded a
new order of sannyāsīs among Rāmakrishna's followers. He travelled in
America, England and India, and was a persuasive preacher.

Amar Chitra Kathā, No. 146.
Sarma, *Hinduim Through the Ages*, 138-57.
The Story of Vivekananda.

2.7.13. *Rabīndranāth Tagore* (1861-1941): Bengali poet. His poems, translated into English, won international fame; he also painted and composed music. His artistic life was intimately linked to his religious life; for, he said,

> My religion is a poet's religion; its touch comes to
> me through the same unseen and trackless channels as
> does the inspiration of my music.

Beauty, love and joy were for him the surest ways through which man can know God. He disliked some aspects of Hinduism, notably blood-sacrifice (see his plays *Sacrifice* and *Malini*) and asceticism (see his play *Sannyasi*), both of which offended against his love for all life. At the same time he loved the Upanishads and popular bhakti poetry. His stories (e.g. *The Golden Boat*) and his *Collected Poems and Plays* present his ideas attractively, and can be used imaginatively in school.

Amar Chitra Kathā, No. 136.
Sarma, *Hinduism Through the Ages*, 157-78.
Tagore, *The Religion of Man*; *Collected Poems and Plays*; *The Golden Boat*.

2.7.14. *Mohandās Karamchand Gāndhī* (1869-1948): a unique figure, perhaps the most widely known Indian next to the Buddha. As a student in London and as a lawyer in South Africa, he found himself called on to explain Hinduism to Westerners, which led him to study it deeply; he formed a life-long attachment to the *Bhagavadgītā*. Returning to India in 1915, he joined the independence movement, bringing with him the techniques of

Vivekānanda

Tagore

non-violent struggle—satyāgraha—and simple living which he had
developed in his campaigns for civil rights for South African Indians.
He recorded these events in *An Autobiography, or the Story of My
Experiments with Truth*.

He held that true religion was the search for truth, since 'Truth is
God'. This search involved abstinence from luxuries, manual labour for
the needs of oneself and one's neighbours, and ahimsā—non-violence
amounting to love for all beings. He saw no boundary between religion
and politics or economics: satyāgraha was not merely a method of re-
solving conflicts but an act of devotion to Truth; hand-spinning was
a religious act as well as a remedy for India's economic dependence on
Britain; and the uplift of the Untouchables was not just a matter of
social reform but a purification of Hinduism.

There is plenty of room for debate on the effectiveness of satyāgraha,
on Gāndhī's views about economics, society, diet and sex, and on his
claim to be a true Hindu. He was accused of cultural backwardness,
inconsistency, an indirect reliance on the threat of violence, a pa-
ternalistic attitude to the Untouchables, and a betrayal of Hinduism;
but he was universally mourned when he was shot by a Hindu extremist.

Sarma, *Hinduism Through the Ages*, 178-98.
Shankar, *The Story of Gandhi*.
Woodcock, *Gandhi*.

2.7.15. *Sarojinī Naidu* (1879-1949): Bengali poet and orator. In 1898
she defied her Bengali Brahmin family by marrying a South Indian non-

brahmin. Though her poetry delighted British critics at first, it is
of a very dated kind; moreover she wrote no more after 1917, becoming
instead an ardent orator and political leader. She was one of Gāndhī's
most devoted associates, and worked for the freedom of India, social
justice and women's rights at public meetings, on deputations to meet
the British authorities, and in jail. Though weak in health, she was
always friendly and courageous.

2.7.16. *Sarvepalli Rādhākrishnan* (1888-1975): philosopher, religious
thinker and statesman. After a distinguished career in Indian universities, he became the first Spalding Professor of Eastern Religions and
Ethics at Oxford, and later President of India. Like Vivekānanda, but
in a more academic way, he sought to bring together Indian and Western
thought on the basis of Advaita Vedānta. He held that the foundation
of religion was mystical experience, and that this experience, whatever
the credal terms in which it was expressed, was experience of the unity
of the self with Brahman. His book *The Hindu View of Life*, originally
a series of lectures in England, shows what he considers most valuable
in the Hindu tradition. He also translated the Upanishads and
Bhagavadgītā.

Sarma, *Hinduism Through the Ages*, 217-45.

2.7.17. *Jawaharlāl Nehru* (1889-1964): the first Prime Minister of the
present Republic of India. Born into a wealthy, highly educated and
politically active Kashmiri brahmin family, he was educated in England,

Gāndhī

Rādhākrishnan

and started his political career as a follower of Gāndhī. He led India
to independence in 1947, and was Prime Minister from then until his deat
He combined zeal for socialism and economic planning with faith in democ
racy and the power of the masses. His attitude to Indian culture is wel
expressed in his book *The Discovery of India*—written, like many books
by Indian politicians, in prison.

Thapar and Spear, *A History of India*, II, 244-56.

3.0. *INTRODUCTION*

While it is possible to use English words like 'God', 'salvation' or 'temple' in talking about Hinduism, we could not have discussed Hinduism as we have in this book without using some of the words used in Indian languages for ideas and things which are unfamiliar in English. Many of these words are explained where they occur, but they are explained again in the glossary, together with some other words which may be met with in further reading or in talking with Hindus.

The dozens of languages in India have different words for religious concepts. However, they all use some words derived from the ancient Indian learned language, Sanskrit, and Sanskrit texts are read by pandits in all parts of India. For this reason, Sanskrit words are used a great deal in discussing Hinduism, and most of the words listed here are Sanskrit. Different Indian languages use different forms and pronunciations of the Sanskrit words (0.3), so you may find Hindus using different forms from the ones given here; North Indians generally leave out the final *a* of Sanskrit words, and say *ved*, *prasād*, not *veda*, *prasāda*. We have kept this *a*, however, except in words that have familiar English forms such as *brahmin*, *pandit*.

Some of the words listed in the glossary come from other Indian languages, and others are not Indian at all, like *caste*, *untouchable*. In such cases we have sometimes given the corresponding Sanskrit word as well.

3.1. *THE SPELLING OF INDIAN WORDS*

Indian languages are written in various scripts which show distinctions not shown by our Roman alphabet. When Indian words are spelt in Roman script in specialist works in English, these distinctions are shown by marks (known as diacritical marks) above and below the letters. These marks do not matter unless one wishes to know the exact pronunciation of a word, or its spelling in the original script.

As this book is not written for specialists, the specialists' spelling is not used, though it is given in brackets in the glossary, and will be met with in many of the books listed in the bibliography (e.g. Basham, *The Wonder That Was India*; Edgerton, *The Bhagavadgītā*. The translation of the *Laws of Manu* in the Sacred Books of the East series uses another system of spelling which has rightly gone out of fashion). Instead, we have used a spelling that we hope will help teachers and pupils to approximate to the sounds of Indian words, without giving them too much to learn.

3.2. THE SPELLING USED IN THIS BOOK, AND HOW TO PRONOUNCE IT

The only mark used in our spelling is the long mark or macron (⁻), to distinguish long vowels from short ones. This is important because the lengths of the vowels make a great difference to the rhythm of a word. Notice the difference between the usual English pronunciation of Himalaya (with the first *a* short and unstressed) and the Indian pronunciation Himālaya (with the first *a* pronounced long as in *father*, and stressed).

The pronunciation of *father* referred to above is the one used in what is known as *Received Pronunciation*. Received Pronunciation (RP) is the one in which most of the English examples below will be given, unless otherwise stated. RP can be briefly described as the only non-regional accent of British English; it is the form of pronunciation most commonly described in works on the phonetics of British English and it is traditionally taught to foreign learners of English. The technical label RP is used here in preference to 'Southern British English' because of the imprecise nature of the latter term, since there are many varieties of Southern British English.

Unmarked vowels

a may be pronounced either like the vowel in RP *but*, or like the vowel in Northern English *bat*.

i is like the vowel in RP *bit*; *Shiva* sounds like RP *shiver*.

u is like the vowel in RP *pull* (never like the vowel in RP *but*).

a, *i*, *u* are *short* vowels.

e is like the vowel in RP *take*. *Veda* rhymes with *invader*, not with *leader* or *header*.

o is like the vowel in RP *boat*; *holi* sounds like RP *holy*.

e and *o* are both *long* vowels, though they are written without a mark. (Most Indian languages have no short *e* or *o*, so a mark would be unnecessary.)

Marked vowels

ā is like the first vowel in RP *father*.

ī is like the vowel in RP *see*.

ū is like the vowel in RP *boot*.

ā, *ī*, *ū* are *long* vowels.

Diphthongs

ai is like the vowel in RP *fine*.

au is like the vowel in RP *now*.

Consonants

ph, *th* are pronounced like the *p* and *t* in RP *pin*, *tin* (*not* as *ph* and *th* in *photograph*, *thin*). *kh* is pronounced as in the first consonant of RP *kill, can.* The *h* in *ph, th, kh* represents a puff of breath.

p, t, k are pronounced as in the second consonants of RP *spin, stint, skill,* without a puff of breath.

bh, dh, gh are like RP *b, d, g,* followed by a puff of breath. However, if this is difficult, pronounce them simply as RP *b, d, g.*

ch is pronounced as in RP *church; chh* is the same followed by a strong puff of breath.

r is always pronounced, even when it comes after a vowel and before a consonant. Try to roll the *r* (as in Scots English) in words like *artha, karman.*

y is always a consonant, never a vowel; *ārya, vaishya, sūrya* have only two syllables each.

In the word *brahman,* the *h* is pronounced, and does not affect the vowel before it, which is short. In *brahmin,* however, the *a* is long (as in *father*) and the *h* need not be pronounced; *brahmin* is an anglicized spelling, the Sanskrit form being *brāhmaṇa.*

j is pronounced as in English *jam* (not as in French *Jean*), except when *n* follows (see *jñāna*).

Stress

An acute accent is used in the glossary to mark the syllable on which the stress falls. Stresses are not marked when the words occur elsewhere in this book.

Finer points of pronunciation are not represented in the spelling used in this book, but only in the specialists' spelling given in brackets in the glossary. These finer points may be found in the pronunciation guides given in some books which use the specialists' spelling (such as Basham, *The Wonder That Was India;* De Bary, *Sources of Indian Tradition;* O'Flaherty, *Hindu Myths*), though such guides are often too brief to be explicit. Alternatively, listen to how Indians pronounce the words; but remember that people from different parts of India will pronounce the same word in different ways. The pronunciation described here is necessarily somewhat anglicized.

3.3. THE LAYOUT OF THE GLOSSARY

Each entry in the glossary contains some or all of the following items of information. The entry *brahmin* is used below as an example.

(a) The headword, italicized, spelt in the form used in this book, e.g.:

    brahmin

(b) Any alternative forms that may be met with elsewhere (the mark ⁻ may often be omitted, but it is given here as an aid to pronunciation), e.g.:

    brāhman

(c) After the opening bracket, the language of origin, e.g.:

    (Skt.

The following abbreviations are used: Bg. = Bengali; H. = Hindi; Skt. = Sanskrit.

(d) The word in that language, in the spelling used by specialists, e.g.:

    brāhmaṇa

(e) The original meaning or the common meaning in that language, if this differs from the explanation; this is in quotation marks followed by the closing bracket, e.g.:

    'belonging to Brahman')

(f) The explanation. In the explanation, numbers, e.g. (2.2.2), refer to sections of this book. Italicized words, e.g. *varna*, refer to other entries in the glossary. Sometimes the letters (a), (b), (c) are used to distinguish two or more meanings of the same word.

āchārya (Skt. ācārya). A teacher, especially the one who initiates a
   boy with the Sacred Thread and teaches him the Veda (2.1.2). Also a
   title for great theologians such as Shankarāchārya 'the teacher
   Shankara', Rāmānujāchārya 'the teacher Rāmānuja'.

Advaita (Skt. Advaita 'free from duality; non-dualist'). The most
   influential school of Vedānta, founded by Shankara, and teaching that
   Brahman is the only reality (2.4.2).

ahimsā (Skt. ahimsā 'harmlessness, non-violence'). A moral principle
   taught in ancient Sanskrit texts. Gāndhī insisted on it, and regarded
   it as not merely abstention from harm but a positive love for all
   beings.

Ambā (Skt. ambā 'mother'). A mother-goddess worshipped in Gujarāt, also
   called Mātājī 'mother', or Ambemātā 'mother Ambā'; she is sometimes
   identified with *Pārvatī* (2.3.0, 2.3.1).

āmrita, *āmrit* (Skt. Amṛta 'not dead; immortal'). The drink of immortality, which the gods won by churning the ocean (2.3.2.1).

āñjali (Skt. añjali). A gesture of respectful greeting, in which the
   hands are placed together, slightly hollowed, and raised to the breast
   or forehead (2.1.1.2); also called *namaskāra*.

āratī (Skt. āratī). Worship by waving a lamp in front of the image
   (2.1.1, 3.1.3).

Ārjuna, *Ārjun* (Skt. Arjuna). A hero, the third of the five Pāndava
   brothers in the *Mahābhārata* (2.5.2), who is Krishna's disciple in the
   Bhagavadgītā.

ārtha (Skt. artha 'purpose; wealth'). The second of the three worldly
   aims of man (see *dharma*); it is the pursuit of worldly success,
   including wealth and political power (2.4.1).

Ārya Samāj (Skt. Ārya-samāja '*Aryan* society'). A religious organization
   founded in 1875 by Dayānanda Sarasvatī (1824-1883), a Gujarātī brahmin
   It teaches that the Vedas are the source of all truth, that there is
   only one God, that he is to be worshipped without the use of idols,
   and that it is the duty of Āryas—that is, of true Hindus—to spread
   this worship throughout the world.

Āryan (Skt. ārya). (a) Name of the people who entered north-west India
   from about 1500 B.C. onwards, among whom the Veda was composed. (b)
   Belonging to the three *twice-born* varnas. The division of people into
   Aryans and non-Aryans originated with the Aryan invasion of north-west
   India, and remains an important part of the traditional Hindu view of
   society (2.2.2, 2.6.2). (The word 'Aryan' was sometimes used in the
   nineteenth century to refer to the whole Indo-European language family,
   and to a supposed race of original speakers of Indo-European languages
   it was later used in the racial theories adopted by the Nazis. These
   meanings are not intended in this book, nor in modern scholarly work
   generally.)

āshrama, *āshram* (Skt. āśrama). (a) The four āshramas are stages through

which a twice-born man passes: student (brahmachári), householder
(grihástha), hermit (vānaprástha) and monk (sannyásin). (b) A place
where a group of people live a holy life, a monastery.

Athárva-Véda (Skt. atharva-veda 'knowledge belonging to a class of
priests called Atharvans). A part of the *Veda* (not always included)
containing spells and prayers for personal benefits (2.5.1).

átman, átma (Skt. ātman 'self'). The self or soul which is present in
all conscious beings. According to *Advaita Vedānta*, there is really
only one Self, which is the same as *Brahman*, and which only appears
to be many; but other systems see the world as populated by a multitude of selves (2.4.1, 2.4.2).

ávatār, avatára (Skt. avatāra 'descent'). A form in which a god,
especially Vishnu, descends into the world: an incarnation (2.3.1,
2.3.2.5)

Ayódhyá (Skt. Ayodhyā). The capital city of King Rāma (2.3.1, 2.5.2).
Its modern name is Faizābād, Awadh or Oudh.

Báli (Skt. Bali). A demon defeated by Vishnu in his dwarf incarnation
(2.1.5.4, 2.3.1).

Behár, Bihár (Skt. vihāra 'Buddhist monastery'). A region of North
India, west of Bengal.

Bengál (Skt. Vaṅga). The region around the lower reaches of Ganges
and Brahmaputra rivers in North-Eastern India; now divided politically
into West Bengal (a province of the Republic of India) and Bangladesh
(which from 1947 to 1971 was East Pakistan).

Bengáli. Belonging to Bengal; the language of Bengal.

Bhágavadgítā (Skt. Bhagavad-gītā 'sung by Krishna'). A religious poem
in Sanskrit, in which Krishna teaches Arjuna; composed in the last
few centuries B.C. and forming part of the *Mahābhārata* (2.4.2, 2.5.2).

Bhágavata Purāna, Bhāgavata, Bhāgavatam (Skt. Bhāgavata-purāṇa). The
best-known of the *Purānas*, containing many myths about Vishnu, including the story of Krishna.

bhájan (Skt. bhajana 'act of devotion'). Song of praise to a god;
devotional meeting for singing, listening to recitation of the god's
exploits, etc.

bhákti (Skt. bhakti). Devotion, love of God. Bhakti is expressed in
poetry, music, dance and painting, or in loving service to an image.
Some bhaktas (devotees) have been so lost in the love of God that they
seemed mad (2.4.1, 2.4.2, 2.7.5).

bílva, vílwa, bel (Skt. bilva). A tree sacred to Shiva; its leaves are
scattered on the linga during pūjā (2.1.5.5).

Bráhmá (Skt. Brahmā). Name of a god (2.3.1).

bráhmachárī, brahmachārin (Skt. brahmacārin). A boy or man who has
been initiated with the Sacred Thread and is studying the Veda; he is
in the first of the four *āshramas*.

bráhmachárya (Skt. brahmacarya). Studentship, the state of being a
brahmachārī. Since a brahmachārī has to take the vows of abstinence,

including chastity, the word is also used to mean abstinence from sex.

Bráhman, Bráhma, Brahm (Skt. Brahman). The eternal being on which all beings depend; the Absolute; God. Perfect knowledge of Brahman is salvation or *moksha* (2.4.1). According to *Advaita Vedānta*, Brahman is identical with the *ātman*.

Bráhmana (Skt. brāhmaṇa 'belonging to Brahman'). A type of text, forming part of the Veda, which describes and explains the ritual.

bráhmin, bráhman (Skt. brāhmaṇa 'belonging to Brahman'). A member of the hereditary priestly class (2.2.2; *varna*). Only brahmins can teach the Vedas and perform certain rituals, including many of the samskāras. About 16% of the Hindu population of India are brahmins.

Bráhmo Samáj (Bg. from Skt. brāhmya-samāja 'society of God'). Religious society founded in 1828 by Rāmmohun Roy (2.7.9).

Búddha (Skt. Buddha 'aware, enlightened'). The title of Siddhārtha Gautama the founder of Buddhism (2.7.1), remembered by Hindus as an avatār of Vishnu.

caste (Portuguese casta 'breed, lineage'). A caste is a hereditary group into which each Hindu is born and within which he can marry (2.2.2). The Sanskrit word for 'caste' is jāti. The whole set of behaviour patterns and social institutions connected with the castes is also called caste. A 'caste Hindu' is a Hindu who observes caste rules and who is not an Untouchable. Some writers use the word 'caste' in the sense of *varna*.

Chaitánya (Skt. Caitanya 'consciousness'). Name of a 16th-century Bengali devotee of Krishna (2.7.5).

dárshana, dárshan (Skt. darśana 'sight, view'). (a) The experience of seeing a god in the form of an image, or in one's mind, or in a vision. People visit temples to have darshana of the god in his image (2.1.3.6); sometimes holy men also give darshana to their devotees by appearing in front of them. (b) Any system of philosophy and theology (2.4.2).

Dásará, Daséra, Dusséhra (Skt. daśaharā). A festival in late September or early October (2.1.5).

Dáyánánda Sarásvatī (Skt. dayānanda 'delighting in compassion'; sarasvatī, name of an order of sannyāsīs). Founder of the Ārya Samāj, lived 1824–1883 (2.4.3).

Déccan (Skt. dakṣiṇa 'right-hand; southern'). The peninsular part of India, excluding the extreme south.

déva (Skt. deva). A god.

dévatā (Skt. devatā). A deity, whether a god or a goddess.

dévī (Skt. devī). A goddess; also a title for brahmin women. The wife of Shiva is sometimes called Devī; see *goddess*.

dhárma (Skt. dharma 'law'). The sacred law which governs Hindu life; also righteousness, action which conforms to the law. Dharma is the highest of the three worldly aims of man; the others are *artha* and *kāma*.

dhárma-shástra (Skt. dharma-śāstra). A law-book; the science of sacred law (2.5.2).

dhótī (H. dhotī). The lower garment of Hindu men, a piece of cloth wrapped round the waist and hanging to the knees, the end being passed between the legs and tucked in at the back of the waist.

Dīwálī (H. Dīwālī); Dīpávali (Skt. Dīpāvali 'row of lamps'). A festival in late October or early November (2.1.5.4).

Dravídian (Skt. drāviḍa 'belonging to South India, Dravidian'). Name of a family of languages (chiefly Tamil, Telugu, Kannada, Malayālam) spoken in South India; there are a few Dravidian languages in the north also. The name is also used for the culture of South India and its features (e.g. 'Dravidian architecture'), and sometimes also for the pre-Aryan peoples generally (2.6.0, 2.6.1).

Dúrgā (Skt. Durgā). Name of *Pārvatī*, the wife of Shiva, particularly as slayer of the buffalo demon (2.1.5.3).

Dúrgā Pújā (Skt. Durgā-pūjā 'worship of the goddess Durgā'). A festival, especially popular in Bengal, in late September or early October (2.1.5.3).

Dusséhra. See *Dasarā*.

dvíja. See *twice-born*.

Gándhī (Skt. gāndhika 'perfume and spice merchant'). Family name in Gujarāt; for M. K. Gāndhī, see 2.7.14).

Ganésha, Ganésh or Gánapati (Skt. Gaṇeśa or Gaṇapati 'leader of the hosts'). Name of the elephant-headed god (2.3.1).

Gánges (Skt. Gaṅgā). The principal river of India; the Ganges basin, running mainly west to east through North India, is the most densely populated part of India. It is the most sacred river in India; it is said to have come down from heaven, and to flow originally from the left big toe of Vishnu (2.3.2.4).

Gáruda (Skt. Garuḍa). The mythical bird on which Vishnu rides (2.3.3).

Gáyatrī Mántra or Sāvitrī (Skt. Gāyatrī Mantra, Sāvitrī). The best-known verse in the Veda, recited in daily prayers and in the Thread-ceremony (2.1.1, 2.1.2, 2.5.1).

ghee (H. ghī; Skt. ghṛta). Butter clarified by boiling away its water content, used in cooking and in worship.

ghāt (H. ghāt). A set of steps down the bank of a river or tank, for embarking, drawing water or bathing (2.1.4).

Gítā (Skt. Gītā). Short for *Bhagavadgītā* (2.5.2).

God, god. When we use a capital *G*, we refer to the one God, the lord of all (Skt. *īśvara*). On the other hand a 'god' with a small *g* is one of many gods (Skt. *deva*) (2.3.0).

goddess. A female god (Skt. devī). 'The Goddess' usually means the wife of Shiva, who has many names; see *Parvatī, Kalī*.

Gókula, Gókul (Skt. go-kula 'cow-community'). The village on the Jumna where Krishna was brought up (2.3.2.5).

Gókulāshtamī (Skt. Gokulāṣṭamī 'eighth of Gokula'). See *Janmāshtamī*.

Gópī (Skt. gopī). A cowherd girl; referring especially to the girls who loved Krishna (2.3.2.5).

gópuram, gópura (Skt. go-pura 'cow castle'). The tower over a South Indian temple gateway, usually covered with sculpture (2.1.3.2).

Góvinda, Góvind (Skt. Go-vinda 'cow-finder'). A name of Krishna.

grihástha (Skt. gṛha-stha 'staying in the house'). A householder, a man in the second of the four *āshramas*, who is married and has the duties of raising sons, worshipping the gods, and studying the Vedas (2.1.2).

Gujarāt, Gujerát (Skt. Gurjara). The north-western part of peninsular India.

Gujarātī. Belonging to Gujarāt; the language of Gujarāt.

gúru (Skt. guru 'heavy; important; venerable'). A teacher, especially one who imparts traditional learning; he is held in the highest respect by his pupils.

Hánuman, Hánumant (Skt. Hanumat 'with jaws'). Name of a monkey chief who helped Rāma (2.5.2). He is worshipped as a god in North India.

Haráppan civilization or Indus Valley civilization. An ancient civiliz-ation discovered by archaeologists in 1922; its best-known sites are Mohenjo-Dāro and Harappā, in the Indus valley. It flourished in north-west India from about 2,500 to 1,500 B.C., and some of its features survive in present-day Hinduism (2.6.1).

Hardwár (Skt. Hari-dvāra 'Vishnu's gate'). A place of pilgrimage, where the Ganges leaves the Himālayas for the plains (2.1.4).

Hárijan (Skt. Hari-jana 'Vishnu's people'). Name given by M. K. Gāndhī to the Untouchables, to show that Hindus should treat them with respect.

hávan (Skt. havana 'pouring'). See *homa*.

Himālaya (Skt. Himālaya 'abode of snow'). The great mountain range which divides India from Central Asia. Often pronounced Himaláya in English.

Hindī (H. Hindī). The language of Hindustān (the central plain of North India). It is the most widely spoken language of India, and is the national language of the Republic of India.

Híndu (Persian Hindū). The name given by the Persians to the river Indus (Skt. Sindhu; our name Indus comes from Persian through Greek and Latin) and the land on and beyond it. The Muslim invaders of India applied this term to the non-Muslim inhabitants, to distinguish them from themselves, and so the term Hindu came to mean people of a particular religion (0.3).

Hólī (Skt. holī, holikā). A spring festival in late February or early March (2.1.5.6). The word is not connected with English *holy*.

hóma (Skt. homa 'pouring'). A form of sacrifice in which a little food is poured into a fire (2.1.1); also called *havan*.

India (Latin, from Persian *Hindū*). (a) The present Republic of India. (b) The whole *subcontinent* south of the Himalayas, which includes Pakistan and Bangladesh. In this book, we use the second meaning except where indicated (0.3, 2.6.0, 2.6.6).

Indo-Áryan. The name given by modern scholars to the family of languages which includes Sanskrit and many of the vernacular languages of India. It is a branch of the *Indo-European* language family (2.6.0).

Indo-Európean. The name given by modern scholars to a large family of languages, which has members in India and in Europe. It includes most of the languages of Europe (all except Basque, Finnish and Hungarian), Persian, and the *Indo-Aryan* languages (2.6.0).

Índra (Skt. Indra). The warrior god of the Vedic Aryans, to whom a quarter of the hymns in the *Rig-Veda* are addressed.

Indus Valley civilization. See *Harrapan civilization.*

íshta-dévatā (Skt. iṣṭa-devatā 'chosen deity' or 'worshipped deity'). The god or goddess whom a Hindu chooses as his chief object of worship.

Íshvara, Íshwar (Skt. īśvara 'lord'). The Lord, God, the ruler of the universe who is higher than the ordinary gods.

Jain (Skt. jaina 'belonging to the conquerors'). The Jains are the members of a religion (Jainism), taught by Mahāvīra around 500 B.C. in the Ganges basin—in the same period and region as the Buddha—and probably going back much further. It lays great stress on *ahimsā*, and flourishes mainly among the merchant classes of Western India.

Janmáshtamī (Skt. janmāṣṭamī 'eighth of the birth'). The festival of Krishna's birthday, on the eighth day of the waning moon in July or early August, also called Gokulāshtamī (2.1.5.2).

jnána (pronounced *nyána*. Skt. jñāna). Knowledge, especially knowledge of the highest truth as a way, or part of the way to salvation (2.4.1).

Júmna, Yámunā (Skt. Yamunā). The main tributary of the Ganges. *Gokula,* where Krishna lived (2.3.2), is on the Jumna.

Kailása (Skt. Kailāsa). A mountain in the Himalayas, the home of Shiva and a place of pilgrimage.

Káli Yúga. See *yuga.*

Kálī (Skt. kālī 'black'). The terrible form of the wife of Shiva (see (2.3.1; *Pārvatī*).

Kálighát (Bg. Kālī-ghāt '*ghāt* of the goddess *Kālī*'). a suburb of Calcutta where there is a famous temple of Kālī.

Kálkī (Skt. Kalkin, Kalki). Name of the tenth avatār of Vishnu, who is to come at the end of the Kali *Yuga* riding on a white horse (or in some versions in the form of a white horse) to kill the wicked with his sword and rescue the righteous so that the Krita Yuga can begin again (2.3.1, 2.4.1).

Káma (Skt. kāma 'desire, pleasure'). (a) The lowest of the three worldly aims of man (see *dharma*); it is the pursuit of pleasure, especially sexual love. (b) The god of love, armed with a sugar-cane bow and flower arrows.

Kánnada, Canaŕese (Kannaḍa). A *Dravidian* language spoken in the central part of peninsular India.

kárman, kárma (Skt. karman 'action, deed'). Action, anything that a person has done. Every act which a person had done has an effect on his life thereafter, either in this life or in a future birth, and every good or bad fortune one receives is a result of previous good or bad karman (2.4.1).

Kárttikéya (Skt. Kārttikeya 'son of the Pleiades'). A name of *Skanda*.

Kérala (Skt. Kerala). A region in the south-west of peninsular India.

Kríshna (Skt. kṛṣṇa 'black'). Name of the best-known avatār of Vishnu (2.3.1, 2.3.2.5).

Kríshna-lílā (Skt. Kṛṣṇa-līlā 'Krishna's game'). The life of Krishna; a play or dance telling the life of Krishna.

Kshátriya (Skt. kṣatriya). A member of the second of the four *varnas*, whose function is kingship and warfare (2.2.2). While some castes (many of them called *Rājpūts*) claim to be kshatriyas, their status is disputed by brahmins.

Kúmbha-Mélā (Skt. kumbha 'jar; the constellation Aquarius'; melā 'assembly'). An assembly of pilgrims which takes place at the full moon of the month Māgha (January-February) once in twelve years, when the planet Jupiter enters Aquarius. The Kumbha-Melā is held at Hārdwār (in the upper reaches of the Ganges), Allāhābād (at the confluence of the Ganges and the Jumna), and Nāsik (in Western India) (2.1.4).

Lákshmana, Lákshman (Skt. Lakṣmaṇa). A younger brother of *Rāma* (a).

Lákshmī (Skt. Lakṣmī). Name of the goddess of wealth, wife of Vishnu (2.3.1).

Lánkā (Skt. Laṅkā). In the *Rāmāyana*, the island ruled by the demon king Rāvana, identified with the modern Sri Lanka (formerly called Ceylon).

línga (pronounced like English *linger*, not to rhyme with *singer*. Skt. liṅga 'mark, feature; sex organ'). The form in which Shiva is worshipped. It is usually carved in stone, cylindrical in shape and rounded at the top (2.3.3).

lotus (Greek lōtos, a word also used for several other plants; the usual Skt. word is *padma*). A pink, blue or white flower like a water-lily.

lotus position (Skt. padmāsana). The commonest posture used in yoga: sit cross-legged with your right foot on your left thigh and your left foot on your right thigh (2.1.1.1).

Mahābhárata (Skt. mahā-bhārata 'the great [poem] belonging to the Bhārata family'). A Sanskrit epic telling the story of a dynastic struggle among the descendants of King Bharata, in which the five sons of King Pāndu are the protagonists; it also contains teachings on dharma and other matters. It is the longest poem in the world, in

100,000 verses, and historians consider it was composed gradually, between about 500 B.C. and 300 A.D.

Mahārāshtra (Skt. mahārāṣṭra 'great territory'). A region in the west of peninsular India.

Mahāshivarātri (Skt. mahā-śiva-rātri 'great night of Shiva'). See *Shivarātri.*

mántra (Skt. mantra). A verse, especially one from the Vedas, used in ritual and having supernatural power.

Mánu (Skt. Manu). Name of an ancestor of mankind who revealed the dharma. A *dharma-shástra,* the *Laws of Manu,* is named after him; it is often called *Manu* for short (2.5.2).

Maráthī. Belonging to *Mahārāshtra*; the language of Mahārāshtra.

Máthurā (Skt. Mathurā). A city on the Jumna, the birthplace of Krishna.

móksha or *múkti* (Skt. mokṣa or mukti 'release'). The Hindu view of salvation, a state of perfect freedom in which there is no cycle of births and deaths (*samsāra*).

Múghal, Mógul (Persian Mughal 'Mongol, Mongolian'). Name of a Muslim dynasty which ruled in Delhi from 1555 to 1858, though its power declined in the mid-eighteenth century. In the Mughal period a distinctive Indian Islamic culture developed.

Múrugan, Múrukan (Tamil Murukaṉ). See Skanda.

nāmadhéya (Skt. nāma-dheya 'name-putting'). The *samskāra* in which a child is given a name (2.1.2).

namaskára, namaskár (Skt. namaskāra 'act of homage'). See *anjali.*

námas té (Skt. namas te 'homage to you'). Words said in greeting, often while making the *anjali* (2.1.1.2).

Nándī, Nándin (Skt. Nandin). The bull who is Shiva's attendant (2.3.3).

Natarájā (Skt. Naṭarājan 'king of dance'). A title of Shiva, whose dancing sets the rhythm of the world in motion. Shiva in this form is the subject of many South Indian sculptures (2.3.3).

Navarátri (Skt. nava-rātri 'nine nights'). The nine-day period in late September or early October which ends with *Dasarā* (2.1.5.3).

Om (Skt. Oṃ). The sacred syllable, also called the Omkāra or the Pranava. The solemn sound Om is pronounced at the beginning of many Hindu prayers (2.1.1).

Pándava (Skt. pāṇḍava 'belonging to Pāṇḍu'). Family name of the five brothers who are the heroes of the *Mahābhārata* (2.5.2; see *Arjuna*).

pándit, púndit (Skt. paṇḍita). A scholar, a learned man, especially one who knows Sanskrit. Used as a hereditary title by some Brahmin families.

Pánjāb, Púnjab (Persian panj āb 'five waters'). A region of northwestern India, watered by five tributaries of the Indus.

Panjábī. Belonging to Panjāb; the language of Panjāb.

Párashurāma, Párashurām (Skt. paraśu-rāma '*Rāma* with the axe'). Name of the sixth avatār of Vishnu, sometimes called simply Rāma. He was a brahmin who massacred the *kshatriyas* as a result of a feud between his father and an overweening king (2.3.2).

Pársī, Pársee (Persian Pārsī 'belonging to Persia'). The Parsis are people of Zoroastrian religion, living mainly in Western India, whose ancestors fled from Iran because of Muslim persecution in the 7th and 8th centuries A.D.

Párvatī (Skt. pārvatī 'daughter of the mountain'). Name of a goddess, the wife of Shiva; also called *Durgā*, *Kālī*, *Umā*, or simply Devī 'the goddess' (2.3.1).

Prahlāda, Prahlád (Skt. prahlāda 'joy'). Name of a legendary devotee of Vishnu (2.3.2.3).

pranāma, pranám (Skt. praṇāma). The act of kneeling and touching the ground with the forehead (2.1.1).

prasāda, prasád, parshád (Skt. prasāda 'grace, favour'). Food that has been placed before an image and is afterwards eaten by worshippers; the god has shown favour by allowing them to eat it (2.1.1, 2.1.3).

pūjā (Skt. pūjā). Worship of a god with offerings and mantras, at the home shrine or in a temple (2.1.1, 2.1.3).

Purāna, Purán (Skt. purāṇa 'ancient'). The purānas are a class of *smriti* texts in Sanskrit. They contain myths, passages in praise of various gods, and instructions on dharma and worship (2.5).

puróhita, puróhit (Skt. purohita 'placed in front'). In Vedic times, the chief priest of an Aryan king; in modern times, a brahmin who performs rituals for a Hindu family (2.2.1).

Rádhā (Skt. Rādhā). The name of Krishna's favourite among the *gopīs*, sometimes said to be a form of *Lakshmī* (2.3.2.5).

Rādhākríshnan (Tamil form of Skt. Rādhā-Kṛṣṇa 'Krishna with Rādhā'). Name of one of the foremost modern Hindu thinkers (2.7.16).

Rájpūt (H. rājpūt, from Skt. rāja-putra 'king's son'). A kshatriya, a person of kingly family; also the name of a race living in Rājasthān (Skt. rāja-sthāna 'place of kings') in North-west India, many of whom have royal titles and fighting traditions.

Ráma, Rām (Skt. rāma 'pleasant'). (a) The name of an ancient king (sometimes called Rāmachandra), the hero of the *Rāmāyana*. He is a model of virtue whose reign was a time of peace and righteousness. He is worshipped as an *avatār* of Vishnu. (b) Rāma is also the name of the elder brother of Krishna, often called Balarāma. (c) See *Parashurāma*.

Rāmachándra (Skt. Rāma-candra 'Rāma-moon'). See *Rāma* (a).

Rāmakríshna (Skt. Rāma-Kṛṣṇa 'Krishna with Rāma'). Name of a nineteenth-century Bengali saint (2.7.11).

Ráma-návamī (Skt. Rāma-navamī 'Rāma's ninth'). The festival of the birthday of *Rāma* (a), on the ninth day of the waxing moon in March or April (2.1.5.1).

Rāmānuja (Skt. Rāmānuja 'younger brother of Rāma', i.e. Krishna, see *Rāma* (b)). Name of a Vaishnava theologian who lived in the 11th-12th centuries A.D. (2.4.2).

Rāmāyana, Rāmāyan (Skt. Rāmāyana). A Sanskrit poem telling the story of *Rāma* (a).

Rām-Chárit-Mánas (H. Rām-carit-mānas 'the holy lake of the acts of Rāma'). A Hindī poem telling the story of Rama (a), by the 16th-century poet Tulsī Dās.

Rāvana, Rāvan (Skt. Rāvana). Name of a demon king of *Lankā*, enemy of Rāma in the *Rāmāyana*.

rebirth (Skt. punar-janman). Hindus believe that we are born and die again and again in different bodies—not only as people but as animals or even gods or demons. The kind of rebirth we get depends on our *karman* or actions performed in previous births (2.4.1).

Rīg-Véda (Skt. rg-veda 'knowledge of hymns'). A part of the *Veda* containing 1,028 hymns to the gods (2.5.1).

rishi (Skt. rsi). A sage, especially one of the legendary sages who heard the eternal Veda and revealed it to men. See *shruti*.

Rúdra. See *Shiva*.

sacred thread (Skt. upavīta, yajñopavīta, pavitra; Bg. poita). A loop of string worn over the left shoulder and hanging down to the right hip, marking a boy or man who has undergone the *Thread-ceremony* and is allowed to learn the Veda.

salvation. See *moksha*.

Sáma-Véda (Skt. sāma-veda 'knowledge of tunes'). A part of the *Veda* containing a selection of verses from the *Rig-Veda*, with tunes (2.5.1).

sámhitā (Skt. samhitā 'collection'). A term applied to each of the four *Vedas*, especially to the part containing the hymns or *mantras*; these parts are called the *Rig-Veda* Samhitā, *Yajur-Veda* Samhitā, etc.

samsāra, samsār (Skt. samsāra 'flow, course'). The state in which we exist in the world, undergoing a constant series of experiences, pleasant and unpleasant, including repeated birth and death (see *rebirth*). This state continues for ever unless one reaches *moksha* (2.4.1).

samskāra, samskār (Skt. samskāra 'process, preparation'). Any ritual which prepares a person for a new phase of his life, such as name-giving or marriage (2.1.2); sometimes also called a 'sacrament'.

sannyāsa, sannyās (Skt. samnyāsa 'throwing down, casting off'). The breaking of all worldly ties on becoming a *sannyāsī*; the state of being a sannyāsī.

sannyāsī, sannyāsin (Skt. samnyāsin 'he who casts off, a renouncer'). A monk, a man who gives up all worldly concerns to seek salvation; he is in the last of the four *āshramas* (a). He often lives a wandering life, but some sannyāsīs live in monasteries. A female sannyāsī is called a sannyāsinī.

Sánskrit (Skt. saṃskṛta 'processed, prepared, cultivated'; compare *saṃskāra*). The ancient language in which much Hindu religious and other learned literature is composed; it has a similar position in India to that of Latin in Europe. Though in general it is a dead language, some pandits speak it as a second language.

Sarásvatī (Skt. sarasvatī 'full of streams'). Name of the goddess of learning and music, wife of Brahmā (2.3.1).

Sarásvatī Pūjā (Skt. Sarasvatī-pūjā 'worship of Sarasvatī'). A period in which *Sarasvatī* is worshipped, on the last three days of *Navarātrī* (2.1.3.5).

sárī, sáree (H. sāṛī). The usual Hindu women's dress consisting of a long cloth wrapped round the waist and then over the upper body.

Sátya Sai Bábā (Skt. satya 'true'; Sai Bābā, name of an earlier teacher of whom Satya Sai Bābā is a reincarnation). A guru (born 1926), revered by his followers as the avatār of God for the present age. A Telugu himself, he has a following among Gujarātī Hindus in Britain (2.6.7).

satyágraha (Skt. satyāgraha 'holding on to truth'). Gāndhī's term for his technique of non-violent struggle; he translated it into English as 'soul-force' (2.7.14).

Sávitri (Skt. savitṛ 'rouser, life-giver'). Name of a Vedic sun-god, who is worshipped in the daily recitation of the *Gāyatrī Mantra* (2.1.1.1).

Sávitrī (Skt. Sāvitrī 'belonging to Savitri'). (a) Another name for the *Gāyatrī Mantra*. (b) Name of the heroine of a story in the *Mahābhārata*, who gave herself to *Yama*, god of death, in exchange for her husband's life.

self. See *ātman*.

Shaíva, Saíva, Shaívite (Skt. śaiva 'belonging to Shiva'). Worshipper of Shiva. The religion of the Shaivas is called Shaivism.

shálgrām (Skt. śālagrāma). An ammonite or fossil shell, spiral in shape; they are sacred to Vishnu.

Shánkara, Shánkar, Sánkara (Skt. Śaṅkara 'causing welfare', a name of Shiva). Name of a philosopher and theologian (2.7.3).

shástra, sástra, sháster (Skt. Śāstra). A branch of learning, a science; a book giving instruction in a particular subject, such as a *dharma-shāstra*.

Shíva, Síva, Shiv, Shib (Skt. Śiva 'auspicious, kind'). Name of a god, also called Rudra, or Mahādeva, 'the great god' (2.1.3).

Shivarátri (Skt. Śiva-rātri 'Shiva's night'). A night of fasting, sacred to Shiva, also called Mahāshivarātri (2.1.5.5).

shrúti (Skt. śruti 'hearing; what is heard'). Another word for *Veda*. This term is used because the Veda, which is eternal, is believed to have been heard, not made up, by the rishis who revealed it. Compare *smṛti*.

shūdra (Skt. śūdra). A member of the lowest of the four *varnas*, whose function is to serve the upper three (2.2.2). The majority of Hindus are shūdras.

Sikh (Panjābī Sikh, from Skt. śiṣya 'pupil, disciple'). Follower of a religion (Sikhism) founded by Nānak in the 16th century (2.7.4).

Sītā (Skt. sītā 'furrow'). Name of the wife of *Rāma*.

Skánda (Skt. skanda 'leap, jump'). Name of a god, son of Shiva and *Pārvatī* (2.3.1), also called Kārttikeya, Murugan or Subrahmanya.

smriti (Skt. smrti 'memory; what is remembered'). A class of literature less ancient and sacred than the Veda; it is not eternal like the Veda, but was made up by gods and sages. It includes the *Mahābhārata*, the *Rāmāyana*, the law-books, and the Purānas. *Shruti* and smriti are the two chief textual authorities in Hinduism.

South Asia. The geographical region which includes India, Pakistan, Bangladesh, Sri Lanka, Nepal and Bhutan; some people include Afghanistan and Burma as well (0.3, 2.6.6).

subcontinent; the Indian subcontinent. This term is often applied to the part of Asia that is separated from the rest by the Himālayas; it thus covers India, Pakistan and Bangladesh. Compare *India* (b) (0.3, 2.6.0, 2.6.6).

Subrahmánya, Subramániam (Skt. subrahmanya 'holy'). See *Skanda*.

Sūrya (Skt. sūrya 'sun'). The god of the sun.

swāmī (Skt. svāmin 'owner, master'). A title for sannyāsīs and other holy men.

Swāminārāyan (Skt. svāmin 'owner, master'; Nārāyana, a name of Vishnu). A Gujarātī teacher, also called Sahajānanda (1781-1830), whose followers consider him an incarnation of God. His religion, a form of Vaishnavism, is promoted by the Swāminārāyan Hindu Mission (2.4.2, 2.6.7).

Tamil. The language spoken by the Tamils in Tamil Nādu in South India. Among the vernacular languages of India, Tamil has the oldest literature, dating back to the first century A.D. In the 7th century A.D., Tamil-speaking saints composed the first vernacular bhakti poetry (2.5.3).

Theosophical Society. A society founded in New York in 1875, to investigate occult knowledge. Claiming links with Hinduism, it moved its headquarters in 1882 to Adyar, near Madras.

thread-ceremony, upanáyana (Skt. upanayana 'bringing near'). The initiation in which a boy of a twice-born caste is given a *sacred thread* to wear and becomes entitled to learn the Veda (2.1.2).

Tirupati, Thírupathi (Tamil Tirupati). A pilgrimage centre in South India. The nearby mountain, Tirumalai, is sacred to Vishnu (2.1.4).

Trimūrti (Skt. tri-mūrti 'having three forms'). A representation of God, having the three faces of Brahmā, Vishnu and Shiva (2.3.1).

tulsī (Skt. tulasī). Basil, a herb sacred to Vishnu and used in his worship.

twice-born (Skt. dvija). A term applied to the first three *varnas* (brahmin, kshatriya and vaishya) because they receive a second birth at the thread-ceremony which entitles them to learn the Veda (2.1.4, 2.2.2).

Umā. See *Pārvatī.*

untouchable (Skt. aspṛśya 'not to be touched'). A term applied to certain castes which are considered so low that their touch or even their presence is polluting to higher castes. Also called depressed castes, scheduled castes (because listed in official schedules in 1931 and 1961), *Harijans.* About 20% of the Hindu population of India are Untouchables.

upanāyana. See *thread-ceremony.*

upánishad (Skt. upaniṣad 'sitting near'). The Upanishads are parts of the Vedas which discuss the origin and nature of man and the universe, and particularly Brahman. They were perhaps called Upanishads because they were first taught by teachers in secret to their closest pupils.

Urdū (Turkish ordū 'camp or court of a nomad chief'). The language developed at the courts of the *Mughals*, resembling Hindi but using many Persian, Arabic and Turkish words and written in Arabic script. It is spoken mainly by North Indian Muslims, and is the national language of Pakistan.

Vaishnava, Vaishnavite (Skt. vaiṣṇava 'belonging to Vishnu'). Worshipper of Vishnu. The religion of the Vaishnavas is called Vaishnavism.

vaishya (Skt. vaiśya). A member of the third of the four *varnas*, whose function is agriculture and commerce (2.2.2). While some castes, often of merchants, claim to be vaishyas, their status is disputed by brahmins.

vānaprástha (Skt. vānaprastha). A forest-dweller or hermit, a man in the second of the four *āshramas.* Though the vānaprastha figures in ancient books such as the *Laws of Manu*, this āshrama is practically obsolete today (2.1.2).

Vārānasi, Benáres (Skt. Vārānasī). A sacred city on the Ganges (2.1.4).

várna (Skt. varṇa 'colour'). The four varnas are the four functional classes (*brahmin, kshatriya, vaishya, shūdra*) of Hindu social theory; sometimes misleadingly called castes (see 2.2.2).

Váruna (Skt. Varuṇa). A Vedic god, guardian of truth and order; in post-Vedic times he has become less important, but is remembered as god of the ocean.

Véda, Ved (Skt. veda 'knowledge'). The collection of texts which Hindus regard as sacred and eternal. It can be called the Veda (singular) or the Vedas (plural), or *shruti* (2.5.1).

Vedánta, Vedánt (Skt. Vedānta 'the end of the Vedas'). This term refers either to the Upanishads, or (more often) to a system of doctrine based on them. There are several schools of Vedānta; they all teach that Brahman is the supreme reality, but they differ in other points (2.4.2).

Védic (Skt. vaidika 'belonging to the Veda'). An adjective indicating that something is connected with the Veda. The 'Vedic Age' is the period when the bulk of the Veda was composed, about 1500-500 B.C.; the 'Vedic Aryans' were the people who composed the Veda; 'Vedic rituals' are rituals prescribed in the Veda. The early form of Sanskrit in which the Vedas were composed is also known as Vedic (2.6.2).

Víshnu (Skt. Viṣṇu). Name of a god (2.3.1).

Vivekánanda (Skt. vivekānanda 'delighting in discrimination'). Name of a great nineteenth-century thinker and preacher (2.7.12).

Vrindávan, Brindában (Skt. vṛndā-vana). The forest where Krishna played, near *Gokula* (2.3.2.5); a centre of pilgrimage, especially for the Chaitanya sect (2.7.5, 2.1.4).

Vyása (Skt. vyāsa 'arranger'). A legendary sage, supposed to have compiled the Vedas and composed the *Mahābhārata*.

Yájur-Véda (Skt. yajur-veda 'knowledge of sacrificial formulae'). A part of the *Veda* containing words spoken by the priest performing ritual actions (2.5.1).

Yáma (Skt. yama 'twin'). Name of the god of death and ruler of the dead.

Yámuná. See *Jumna*.

yóga (Skt. yoga 'yoking; discipline'). Self-discipline, involving meditation and bodily training, with the ultimate aim of *moksha* (2.4.1). There is a Yoga system of beliefs, set out in the Yoga-Sūtras of Patanjali (5th century A.D. or earlier).

yógī, yógin (Skt. yogin 'he who has yoga'). A man who practices *yoga*. A female yogī is called a yoginī.

yúga (Skt. yuga 'yoke; team; age'). The world passes repeatedly through a cycle of four yugas or ages: Krita Yuga, Tretā Yuga, Dvāpara Yuga and Kali Yuga. We are now in the Kali Yuga, which is the worst of the four (2.4.1). The word Kali is not connected with the name Kālī.

4.0. *NOTES ON THE BIBLIOGRAPHY*

This bibliography lists all the works referred to in this book, and others which are recommended. Those described as 'class' books are suitable for distribution to the class as textbooks; the others are more suitable for the school library. Indications of age-group are only suggestions.

The following symbols and abbreviations are used in the bibliography:

1	suitable for ages 5-7
2	suitable for ages 7-9
3	suitable for ages 9-11
4	suitable for ages 11-13
5	suitable for ages 13-16
6	suitable for the sixth form
T	suitable for the teacher
ed.	editor
edn.	edition
o.p.	out of print
pb.	paperback
tr.	translator; translated by

Some of the books listed are out of print; where possible, we have indicated this. Some of these books may be reprinted later, not necessarily by the same publisher.

Titles of books are in italics; titles of articles are in quotation marks.

4.1. BIBLIOGRAPHY

Alphonso-Karkala, J. B., *An Anthology of Indian Literature*. Harmondsworth, Penguin, 1971. Includes excerpts from religious texts. T, 6.

Amar Chitra Katha ('Immortal picture stories'). Series of comics for Indian children, on lives of legendary and historical figures. Available from International Publishing Company (4.3). 1-3.

Anantha Murthy, U. R., *Samskara: A Rite for a Dead Man*, tr. A. K. Ramanujan, Delhi, OUP pb., 1976. Outstanding novel, taking some traditional Hindu themes and turning them in surprising directions. For the adventurous who already know something of Hinduism; the translator's notes are helpful. T, 6.

Archer, W. G., *The Loves of Krishna*. London, Allen & Unwin, 1958, o.p. Good survey of Krishna myth, illustrated by eighteenth-century Indian paintings. T, 6.

Asian Directory and Who's Who, The. London, *The Asian Observer*, 1978. Reference book on Asian organizations in Britain, including temples. T.

Bahree, Patricia, *The Hindu World*. London, Macdonald Educational, 1983. Easy to read, excellent colour photographs. 3-5.

Bahree, Patricia, *India, Pakistan and Bangladesh: A Teacher's Handbook*. London, School of Oriental and African Studies, 1982. Much resource and background material, on history, geography and religion. T.

Banerji, Bibhutibhushan, *Pather Panchali: Song of the Road*, tr. T. W. Clark and T. Mukherji. London, Allen & Unwin, 1968. Novel of childhood in rural Bengal, the source of Satyajit Ray's film. T, 6.

Basham, A. L. (ed.), *A Cultural History of India*, London, OUP, 1975. Chapters by leading authorities, on subjects from the Harappan civilization to the present day, including religion. T, 6.

Basham, A. L., 'Hinduism', in R. C. Zaehner (ed.), *The Concise Encyclopaedia of Living Faiths*, London, Hutchinson, 1959; reprinted Boston (U.S.A.), Beacon Press. One of the best short surveys. T, 5-6.

Basham, A. L., *The Wonder That Was India*. 3rd edn., London, Sidgwick & Jackson, 1967. Authoritative survey of ancient Indian culture, to A.D. 1,000. T, 6.

Bhagavadgītā
    Edgerton, F., *The Bhagavadgītā*. Cambridge, Mass., Harvard University Press, 2 vols., 1944; pb., 1974. The most accurate translation, with a full introduction but very little commentary. T, 6.
    Mascaró, Juan, *The Bhagavad Gita*. Harmondsworth, Penguin pb., 1962. Readily available translation, popular but unnecessarily free. T, 6.
    Zaehner, R. C., *The Bhagavadgītā*. London, OUP, 1961; pb. 1973. Translation with introduction and commentary, full and useful. T, 6.
    See also Zaehner, *Hindu Scriptures*.

Boothalingam, Mathuram, *The Children's Ramayana*. Delhi, Publications Division, Ministry of Information and Broadcasting, Government of India, 1967. Illustrated retelling of the epic. 3-4.

Bowen, D. G. (ed.), *Hinduism in England*. London, Darton, Longman & Todd, 1983. A useful collection of papers on Hindu communities in Bradford, Coventry and Leeds, T, 6.

Bridger, Peter, *A Hindu Family in Britain*. Oxford, REP Pergamon, 1969. Introduction to Hinduism and Hindu immigrant culture. 3-5.

Brockington, J. L., *The Sacred Thread: Hinduism in Its Continuity and Diversity*. Edinburgh, Edinburgh University Press, 1981. Comprehensive historical survey. T, 6.

Butler, Donald G., *Life among Hindus* (Friends and Neighbours series). London, Edward Arnold, 1980. Eight short plays dealing with life in the Hindu home, suitable for use with small groups. 4-5.

Butler, Donald G., *Teaching Yoga*. London, Pelham Books, 1980. Teacher's guide to Hatha-Yoga—the form of yoga popular in the West, which emphasizes postures and breathing exercises as well as meditation. T.

Calendar of Religious Festivals. London, Commission for Racial Equality, distributed by Shap Working Party (4.3). Useful guide, published annually, enabling the class to follow the festivals round the year. 4-6.

Clark, Leonard, *Tales from the Panchatantra*. London, Evans Bros., 1979. Well told; imaginative illustrations. 3-4.

Clements, R. D., *God and the Gurus*. Brief and ultimately hostile introduction to three modern Hindu missions to the West, from Christian evangelistic viewpoint. T, 5-6.

Cole, W. Owen, *Five Religions in the Twentieth Century*. Amersham, Hulton, 1981. Topics organized thematically, e.g. 'Worship', 'Festivals'. Suitable for CSE and O-level. 5-6.

Cole, W. Owen (ed.), *Religion in the Multifaith School*. Amersham, Hulton, 1983. Handbook with examples of work and resource lists, a revised edition of a book previously published by Yorkshire Committee for Community Relations. T.

Cole, W. Owen (ed.), *World Religions: A Handbook for Teachers*. London, Commission for Racial Equality, 1977. Hinduism section (pp. 59-94) includes lists of books and resources. T.

Crompton, Yorke, *Hinduism*. London, Ward Lock Educational, 1971. Brief survey by a convert; class book for upper secondary school. T, 5-6.

De Bary, W. T. (ed.), *Sources of Indian Tradition*, 2 vols., pb. New York, Columbia University Press. Anthology of readings, ancient and modern, with introductions. T, 6.

Desai, Anita, *Games at Twilight*. Harmondsworth, Penguin, 1982. Short stories, mainly of middle-class India. T, 6.

Desai, Anita, *Village by the Sea*. London, Heinemann, 1982. Outstanding novel of Indian life for children. 3-5.

Dimock, Edward C., and Levertov, Denise, *In Praise of Krishna*. New York, Doubleday, 1972. Bengali devotional poetry, well translated with illuminating introduction. T, 5-6.

Divali and Other Aspects of Hinduism. Published by and available from
  Resource Centre for Multiracial Education, Peterborough, 1981. Comprehensive details of important aspects of Hindu worship, together
  with advice for teachers. T.

Dutt, Romesh Chandra, *The Ramayana and the Mahabharata.* London,
  Everyman. Abridged Victorian verse versions of the two great
  Sanskrit epics. T, 5-6.

Embree, Ainslie T., *The Hindu Tradition.* Similar in plan to De Bary,
  but a different selection. T, 6.

Ewan, John, *Understanding Your Hindu Neighbour.* London, Lutterworth,
  1977. Much information on Gujarati Hindu family life. 4-5.

Farquhar, J. N., *Modern Religious Movements in India.* London, 1915;
  reprinted Delhi, Munshiram Manoharlal, 1967; New York, International
  Publications Service, 1977. Detailed, full up to its date; not yet
  superseded. A good reference guide. T, 6.

Farquhar, J. N., *An Outline of the Religious Literature of India.*
  London, 1920; reprinted Delhi, Munshiram Manoharlal, 1967; o.p.
  Detailed historical guide and reference book. T, 6.

Gāndhī, M. K., *An Autobiography, or the Story of My Experiments with
  Truth.* Boston (U.S.A.), Beacon Press, 1957. Up to the beginning of
  his Indian political career. Passages could be used for discussion
  of his views, methods and personality. T, 6.

Grant, Eva, *A Cow for Jaya.* Tadworth, World's Work, 1973; o.p. Modern
  made-up story of village life, with good pictures. 1-3.

Hannisford, Janis, *Holi* (Living Festivals series). Exeter, Religious
  and Moral Education Press, 1983. Description of practices; stories
  connected with the festival; activities for the class. Illustrated.
  3-4.

Harrison, Stephen W., *Hinduism in Preston.* Lancaster, Lancashire
  Education Committee, 1978. Study of a Hindu community in Britain. T.

Herod, F. G., *What Men Believe.* London, Methuen, 1968. Class book for
  14+; pp. 8-29 on Hinduism. 5.

Hinduism (Life Educational Reprints No. 80), New York, Life Educational
  Program. Magazine-style presentation, useful for pictures. 1-5.

Hinnells, J. R. & Sharpe, E. J. (ed.), *Hinduism.* Newcastle upon Tyne,
  Oriel Press, 1972. Accounts of aspects of Hinduism, papers on teaching Hinduism, useful bibliography and AVA guide. T.

Hopkins, Thomas J., *The Hindu Religious Tradition* ('The religious life
  of man' series). Encino, California, Dickenson Publ. Co. Inc., 1971.
  Brief, introductory historical survey. T, 6.

How a Hindu Prays. Available from Minority Group Support Service (4.3).
  Specially written and illustrated for young children. 2-3.

Ions, Veronica, *Indian Mythology.* London, Hamlyn, 1967; reprinted
  Newnes, 1983. Some history of religion as well as mythology. Good
  pictures; fairly adult language. T, 6.

Ions, Veronica, *Myths and Legends of India*. London, Hamlyn, pb., 1970;
o.p. Stories from vernacular sources. T, 6.

Jackson, Robert (ed.), *Perspectives on World Religions*. London, School
of Oriental and African Studies, 1978. Curriculum handbook resulting
from SOAS's Teacher Fellowship programme in World Religions. Chapters
on 'Hinduism in religious education' by S. Weightman; 'Social aspects
of Hinduism' by H. Kanitkar. T.

Jackson, Robert (ed.), *Approaching World Religions*. London, John
Murray, 1982. Discussion of issues involved in teaching World
Religions. T.

James, Alan, and Jeffcoate, Robert, *The School in the Multicultural
Society: A Reader*. London, Harper and Row, 1981. Papers on education
in multiracial Britain. T.

Kanitkar, Helen, and Jackson, Robert, *Hindus in Britain*. London, School
of Oriental and African Studies, 1982. Informative accounts about
Hindu communities in Britain, and suggestions for classroom material
and approaches in primary and secondary schools. T.

Keskar, Sharad, *Tales the Ramayana Tells*. Bombay, India Book House
Educational Trust, 1973. Retelling for young children. 3-4.

Khan, N. J., *Twenty Jātaka Tales*. London, East-West Publications (U.K.)
1976. Tales of the former lives of the Buddha. 1-4.

Killingley, D. H., 'Hinduism, tolerance and community education', in
British Journal of Religious Education, summer 1984. Discusses place
of Hinduism in school curriculum and in British life. T.

Killingley, D. H., 'What about caste?', in *Bulletin of the Association
for Religious Education*, Vol. 11, No. 29 (Nov. 1978), 16-18, 13-14.
Introduction to some aspects of caste. T.

Klostermaier, Klaus, *Hindu and Christian in Vrindaban*. London, SCM,
1970; o.p. Vivid account of a well-informed Christian monk's contact
with Hinduism; one of the best books for getting the feel of Hinduism.
T, 6.

Laws of Manu. See Manu.

Leela, S., *Fables from the Panchatantra*. Bombay, India Book House
Educational Trust, 1968. Retold fables, for young children. 1-3.

Lefever, H., *One Man and His Dog*. London, Lutterworth, 1973. Hindu
and Buddhist stories. 3-4.

Mahābhārata. See Dutt; Narasimhan; Picard; Raghavan; Rajagopalachari;
Seeger.

Mahadevan, T. M. P., *Outlines of Hinduism*. Bombay, Chetana, 1977. A
believer's account, written for Hindus but giving useful insights for
the outsider. Teachers and older children. T, 6.

Mahadevan, T. M. P., *Ten Saints of India*. Bombay, Bhāratīya Vidyā
Bhavan, 1961. Lives of six Tamil saint-poets, plus Shankara,
Rāmānuja, Rāmakrishna and Ramana Maharshi, told by a devoted South
Indian scholar. T, 6.

Mandelbaum, D. G., *Society in India*. 2 vols., Berkeley, University of

California Press, 1970. The best comprehensive treatise, useful for a teacher wishing to deepen his knowledge of family, caste and village. T.

Manu (mythical author)
Bühler, George (tr.), *The Laws of Manu* (Sacred Books of the East series, No. 25), Oxford, 1886; reprinted Delhi, Motilal Banarsidass. Standard translation of the best-known dharma-shāstra. T, 6.

Marsh, Howard, *Divali* (Living Festivals series). Exeter, Religious and Moral Education Press, 1983. Description of practices; stories connected with the festival; activities for the class. Illustrated. 3-4.

Mehta, Rām, *Ramu*. London, Angus and Robertson, 1968. A story about Dīvālī. 3.

Michell, George, *The Hindu temple*. London, Paul Elek, 1977. A full, well illustrated study. T.

Mitchell, A. G., *Hindu Gods and Goddesses*. London, H.M.S.O., 1982. Introduction to Hindu iconography, based on bronzes in the Victoria and Albert Museum; 80 plates. T, 6.

Mohanti, Prafulla, *My Village, My Life*. London, Corgi, 1975. Autobiographical look at traditional Hindu life. T, 6.

Narasimhan, C. V. (tr.), *The Mahabharata: an English Translation Based on Selected Verses*. New York, Columbia University Press, 1973. The world's longest poem, shortened by keeping to the main narrative of the dynastic struggle between the five sons of King Pāndu and their cousins. T, 5-6.

Nārāyan, R. K., *Gods, Demons and Others*. London, Heinemann, 1965. Retelling of Hindu myths, with an account of the Indian story-telling tradition, by a major Indian novelist. T, 5-6.

Nārāyan, R. K., *The Guide: A Novel*. Harmondsworth, Penguin, 1980. The anti-hero unintentionally becomes a saint. This and other novels by Nārāyan are intelligent fun and give insight into South Indian life. T, 6.

Nehru, Jawaharlāl, *The Discovery of India*. Bombay, Asia Publishing House, 1965; o.p. A personal and loving view of India's past, by her first prime minister. T, 6.

Nigosian, S. A., *World Religions*. London, Edward Arnold, 1974. Class book for secondary school: pp. 103-38 are on Hinduism. 4.

Niveditā, Sister, *Cradle Tales of Hinduism*. Calcutta, Advaita Ashrama; available from Ramakrishna Vedanta Centre (4.3). Retellings by an early twentieth-century convert. 1-3.

Nowicki, Vivien, 'Hindu festivals', *Bulletin of the Association for Religious Education*, Vol. 2, Nos. 27 and 28 (July 1978).

O'Flaherty, W. D., *Hindu Myths*. Penguin Classics, 1975. Translated from Sanskrit, not retold; therefore difficult. A challenge for teacher and sixth-formers. T, 6.

Panchatantra
Ryder, Arthur W. (tr.), *The Panchatantra*. Bombay, Jaico pb., 1949.

Lively translation of the fullest version of this collection of tales, some cruel, some tender, some bawdy. T, 4-6.
See also Clark; Leela.

Pandey, R. B., *Hindu Saṃskāras*. 2nd edn., Delhi, Motilal Banarsidass, 1969; reprinted Livingston, New Jersey, Orient Book Distributors, 1976; o.p. A description of the life-cycle rituals, including the textual authorities for them. T, 6.

Panikkar, Raimundo, *The Vedic Experience*. London, Darton, Longman and Todd, 1977. Translations, with evocative but verbose commentary, from a wide range of texts. Luxury for secondary school library. T, 6.

Parrinder, E. G., *A Book of World Religions*. Amersham, Hulton Educationa Publications, 1965. Class book. 4-5.

Parrinder, E. G., *The Indestructible Soul*. London, Allen & Unwin, 1973. Introduction to Indian views on immortality; useful as a brief guide to the Upanishads. T, 6.

Picard, B. Leonie, *The Story of the Pandavas*. London, Dobson, 1968; o.p. Retelling of the Mahābhārata for younger readers. 3-4.

Picard, B. Leonie, *The Story of Rama and Sita*. London, Harrap, 1960; o.p. Retelling of the Rāmāyana for younger readers. 3-4.

Rādhākrishnan, S., *The Hindu View of Life*. London, Allen & Unwin, 1927; reprinted Unwin pb., 1960. A modern Hindu philosopher's presentation of ideal Hinduism; originally lectures in England. T, 6.

Rāghavan, V., *The Indian Heritage*. 2nd edn., Bangalore, Indian Institute of World Culture, 1958; o.p. Useful anthology from Sanskrit religious literature, including abridged versions of *Mahābhārata* and *Rāmāyana*. T, 5-6.

Rajagopālāchāri, C., *The Mahābhārata*. Bombay, Bharatiya Vidya Bhavan pb., 1952; reprinted Greenleaf Books, 1980. Free, abridged translatio a useful source of stories. T, 5-6.

Rajagopālāchāri, C., *The Rāmāyana*. Bombay, Bharatiya Vidya Bhavan pb., 1976. Free, abridged translation; a useful source of stories; cheap. T, 5-6.

Raju, P. T., *The Philosophical Traditions of India*. London, Allen & Unwin, 1971. An outline of the philosophical and theological schools. T, 6.

Rāmakrishna, *Sayings of Sri Ramakrishna*. Calcutta, Advaita Ashrama. Oral teachings, often in story form, by the nineteenth-century Bengali saint. T, 4-6.

Ramakrishna for Children. Calcutta, Advaita Ashrama. 2-4.

Rāmānujan, A. K., *Speaking of Śiva*. Harmondsworth, Penguin, 1973. Kannada devotional poetry, in good verse translation, with excellent introduction. T, 5-6.

Rāmāyana
See Boothalingam; Dutt; Keskar; Picard; Rāghavan; Rājagopālāchāri.

Rig-Veda
O'Flaherty, W. D. (tr.), *The Rig Veda*. Harmondsworth, Penguin, 1981.

Selection of hymns, well translated. T, 6.
See also Zaehner, *Hindu Scriptures*.

Sarma, D. S., *Hinduism through the Ages*. Bombay, Bharatiya Vidya Bhavan pb., 1961. Brief history, from Vedic age but giving more space to 19th and 20th centuries. T, 6.

Seeger, Elizabeth, *The Five Sons of King Pandu*. London, Dent, 1970. Retelling of the *Mahābhārata* for young children. 1-4.

Seeger, Elizabeth, *The Ramayana*. London, Dent, 1975. Suitable for the older child. 4-5.

Sen, K. M., *Hinduism*. Harmondsworth, Penguin, 1961. A rather idealized presentation, by a disciple of Rabindranath Tagore. T, 5-6.

Shakuntalā Devī, *Gods and Goddesses in Indian Mythology*. Bombay, India Book House, 1979. Brief but sound descriptions, illustrated. T, 5-6.

Sharma, Ursula, *Rampal and His Family*. London, Collins, 1971; o.p. Life of Panjabi Hindus in India and England, told from tape recordings. T, 6.

Sharpe, E. J., *Thinking about Hinduism*. London, Lutterworth, 1971. Class book. 4.

Sherratt, B. W. and Hawkin, D. J., *Gods and Men: a Survey of World Religions*. London, Blackie, 1972. Class book; pp. 103-48 are on Hinduism. 4-5.

Siek, Marguerite, *Favourite Stories from India*. Hong Kong, Heinemann Asia, 1975. Easy-to-read stories from *Panchatantra, Rāmāyana*, etc. 3-4.

Srīnivās, M. N., *Caste in Modern India*. Bombay, Asia Publishing House, 1962. Collection of articles by a leading Indian anthropologist. T, 6.

Stevenson, Mrs. Sinclair (Margaret Stevenson), *The Rites of the Twice-born*. London, 1920; reprinted Delhi; o.p. Detailed account of Gujarati Brahmin ritual; the rather patronising missionary asides can be ignored. A mine of information for the teacher. T, 6.

Story of Vivekananda, The. Calcutta, Advaita Ashrama. 5.

Stutley, M. and Stutley, J., *A Dictionary of Hinduism*. London, Routledge and Kegan Paul, 1977. Patchy, but the best available encyclopaedia of the Sanskrit tradition. T, 6.

Tagore, Rabīndranāth, *Collected Poems and Plays*. London, Macmillan, 1936. One of the best-known internationally of modern Indian writers; he expresses enduring Hindu values while protesting against some aspects of Hinduism. T, 5-6.

Tagore, Rabīndranāth, *The Golden Boat*. Bombay, Jaico pb. Brief but significant fantasy-stories. 2-5.

Tagore, Rabīndranāth, *The Religion of Man*. London, Unwin pb., 1961. A personal view—useful for enterprising sixth-formers. T, 6.

Tales from Ramakrishna. Calcutta, Advaita Ashrama. Stories with a purpose, told by the 19th-century Bengali saint. 4-5.

Taylor, J. H., *The Half-way Generation: A Study of Asian Youths in*

Newcastle upon Tyne. Windsor, NFER-Nelson, 1976. Surveys attitudes and behaviour of Hindus, Muslims and Sikhs from Panjab. T.

Tambs-Lyche, G. H., *The London Patidars.* London, Routledge and Kegan Paul, 1980. Anthropological study of a Gujarati community. T.

Temples of India. Publications Division, Ministry of Information and Broadcasting, Government of India. Well-illustrated brief guide. T, 4-6.

Temples of North India. Publications Division, Ministry of Information and Broadcasting, Government of India. Well-illustrated brief guide. T, 4-6.

Temples of South India. Publications Division, Ministry of Information and Broadcasting, Government of India. Well-illustrated brief guide. T, 4-6.

Thapar, Romila, *Indian Tales.* London, Bell, 1961. Illustrated. 3-4.

Thapar, Romila, and Spear, Percival, *A History of India.* 2 vols., Pelican pb., 1965-6. A useful handbook to the historical background. T, 6.

Thomas, M. M., *The Acknowledged Christ of the Indian Renaissance.* London, S.C.M., 1969. Surveys modern Hindu thinkers with special reference to their views on Jesus. T, 6.

Thomas, Paul, *Epics, Myths and Legends of India.* Bombay, Taraporewala; reprinted International Publications Service, 1979. Retelling, with illustrations from Hindu images. T, 5-6.

Thomas, Paul, *Festivals and Holidays of India.* Bombay, Taraporewala, 1971; reprinted J. K. Publications, 1979. Comprehensive illustrated survey, covering major religions of India, including Christianity. T, 5-6.

Trudgian, Ray, *Who is My Neighbour?* Nutfield (Surrey), Denholm House Press, 1977. Illustrated introduction to religious activities in multicultural Britain. 4-5.

Upanishads
 Hume, R. E. (tr.), *Thirteen Principal Upanishads.* 2nd edn., London, OUP, 1931. The most accurate translation, with helpful introduction T, 6.
 Mascaró, Juan (tr.), *The Upanishads.* Harmondsworth, Penguin, 1965. Readily available translation, but unnecessarily free.
 Parrinder, E. G., *The Wisdom of the Forest.* London, Sheldon Press, 1975. Selections from the Upanishads. T, 5-6.
 See also Zaehner, *Hindu Scriptures.*

Vivekānanda, Swāmī, *The Complete Works of Swami Vivekananda.* 8 vols., Calcutta, Advaita Ashrama, 1964-1970. Mainly talks, often provocative by an influential late nineteenth-century teacher. T, 6.

Walker, Benjamin, *The Hindu World: An Encyclopaedic Survey of Hinduism.* 2 vols., London, Allen & Unwin, 1968; o.p. Useful in parts, but with concentration on the grotesque. T, 6.

Wigley, B., and Pitcher, R., *Paths to Faith* (The Developing World series), London, Longman, 1970. Thematic treatment of world religions, well illustrated. Pp. 17-20, 24 have some material on Hinduism.   3-4.

Woodcock, George, *Gandhi* (Fontana Modern Masters pb. series), London, Collins, 1972.   Good brief survey.   T, 6.

Yogeshananda, Swami, *The Way of the Hindu*.   Amersham, Hulton Educational Publications, 1973.   Class book.   4.

Zaehner, R. C., *Hinduism*.   London, OUP, pb. 1966.   Learned ideas rather than popular beliefs and practices; a personal but deeply thought out view.   T, 6.

Zaehner, R. C., *Hindu Scriptures*.   London, Everyman pb., 1966.   Translations of a few Vedic hymns, the principal Upanishads and the *Bhagavadgītā*.

Zinkin, Taya, *India and Her Neighbours*.   London, OUP, 1967.   Class book on history and geography of South Asia.   3-4.

It is impossible to list all the films, filmstrips, slides, posters and recordings that become available from time to time; a few are given her to exemplify the variety. For further ideas, visit the places listed i 4.3, or write for their catalogues. Where addresses are not given here see 4.3.

BBC audio-cassettes. Recordings from schools programmes include:
Festivals—Hindu, from Religious Education series, January 1976. 5.
A Hindu Community in Britain, from Religion and Life series, October 1979. 6.
Navaratri, from Quest series, Spring 1981. 3-4.

Cave Temples (Hindu). 11-minute film on rock-cut temple architecture. Guild Sound and Vision. 5-6.

Devi. 93-minute 16 mm. film, in Bengali with English subtitles, by Satyajit Ray. Tragic story of a girl who is believed to be an incarnation of the Goddess. British Film Institute. 6.

Encounter with Hinduism. Filmstrip with tape. BBC Radiovision. 5-6.

Festival Time. 10-minute colour film on Holī, Janmāshtamī, Ganesha's birthday, Dasarā, Dīwālī. Guild Sound and Vision. 3-5.

Hindu Festivals. Set of four wallcharts, each on a festival, with teacher's notes. Pictorial Charts Educational Trust. 3-5.

Hindu Iconography Pack. Four pictures from this book (Vishnu, Lakshmī, Ganesha, Sarasvatī), A4 size suitable for colouring, with notes. £1.50 post free direct from Grevatt & Grevatt, 9 Rectory Drive, Newcastle upon Tyne, NE3 1XT (cash with orders: crossed cheques/ postal orders payable to Grevatt & Grevatt). 3-4.

A Hindu Puja. Filmstrip with tape. Educational Productions. 5-6.

Hinduism. 65-frame filmstrip with tape or cassette and teacher's notes Good pictures of thread-ceremony and worship, with sugary American commentary; younger children would need a different commentary. Concordia Films Ltd., 117/123, Golden Lane, London EC17 8TL. 2-6.

Hinduism. 49-frame filmstrip on gods, worship, pilgrimage, etc. Educational Productions. 3-5.

Hinduism. Filmstrip with tape in two parts with nearly 100 frames; material overlaps with Life Educational Program's book *Hinduism* (4.1) Could be used for younger children with a different commentary instea of the tape. Time-Life. 5-6.

Hinduism. 43-frame filmstrip or slide set. Hugh Baddeley Productions, available from NAVA (4.3). 3-4.

Hinduism: Goddesses and Minor Gods and *Hinduism: The Three Great Gods.* Leaflets, useful for display. British Museum. 4-6.

Hinduism Slide Sets. Over a dozen sets, including *Introduction to Hindu Mythology* (48 slides), *Siva* (24 slides), *Mahatma Gandhi* (12 slides). Ann and Bury Peerless. 4-6.

Holi. Filmstrip with tape, from the Quest series. Shows the festival at the Sri Krishna temple, Coventry. BBC Radiovision. 3.

The Tiger, the Brahman and the Jackal (Folk Tales from Many Lands
  series). 17-frame filmstrip or slides, with notes. Educational
  Productions Ltd. 1-3.

Who is My Neighbour? (Searching for Meaning series). 12 slides, on
  Holī in Coventry. Concord Films Council. 3-4.

Ann and Bury Peerless, 22 King's Avenue, Minnis Bay, Birchington, Kent, CT7 9QL. Sets of slides, with notes, on Hinduism and other Indian subjects. Particularly useful for Hindu temples, shrines and holy places, and for iconography.

Asian Resources Centre, 45 Museum Street, London WC1A 1LR. Catalogues and aids for the multicultural classroom.

Association for Religious Education, 17 Clover Close, Oxford, OX2 9JH. Publishes *Bulletin of the Association for Religious Education*, which often includes articles on aspects of teaching Hinduism and reviews of new material.

Books from India (UK) Ltd., 45 Museum Street, London WC1A 1LR. Importer and retailers of Indian books, including comic strips and other children's books, in English and Indian languages.

BBC Publications, School Orders Section, 144-152 Bermondsey Street, London SE1 3TH. BBC Radiovision filmstrips and tapes; annual list of programmes.

British Film Institute, 81, Dean Street, London W1V 6AA. Films for hire

British Museum, Great Russell Street, London WC1. Pictures, leaflets and books.

Commission for Racial Equality, Elliott House, 10/11 Allington Street, London SW1E 5EH. Its journal *New Community* sometimes has information on Hinduism in Britain. CRE also produces a list, *Ethnic Minority Organizations*, which contains many useful addresses.

Department of Arts Education, University of Warwick, Coventry, CV4 7A Publishes *Resource*, a journal for teachers of religious and moral education (80p per copy post free) with interesting articles and reviews of new material, e.g. Vol. 5, No. 1 (1982): Festival of Indi number.

Educational Productions Ltd., 212 Whitchurch Road, Cardiff, CF4 3NB.

Federation of Hindu Organizations in Great Britain, 74 Cranwell Road, London SW19. Information on Hindu groups.

Gohil Emporium, 366 Stratford Road, Birmingham B11. Images and other articles from India.

Guild Sound and Vision, Woodston House, Oundle Road, Peterborough, PE2 9PZ.

High Commission of India, India House, Aldwych, London WC2. A mine of information; films lent free of charge.

Independent Publishing Company, 38 Kennington Lane, London SE11 4LS. Importers and retailers of Indian books, including comic strips and other children's books, in English and Indian languages; also greetings cards and posters.

Indian Government Tourist Office, 21 New Bond Street, London W1 ODY. Posters and brochures on places of interest, including religious centres.

Minority Group Support Service, Coventry Education Authority, Southfields Old School, South Street, Coventry, CV1 5EJ. Publishes educational material.

National Association for Multi-Racial Education (NAME), 23 Doles Lane, Findern, Derby, DE6 6AX.

National Audio-Visual Aids Library (NAVA), Paxton Place, Gipsy Road, London SE27 2SR. Expensive films for hire at modest charges; its catalogue lists many films on aspects of Hinduism.

National Council of Hindu Temples (UK), c/o Shree Sanatan Mandir, Weymouth Street, Leicester, LE4 6FP.

Open University Educational Enterprises Ltd., 12 Cofferidge Close, Stony Stratford, Milton Keynes, MK11 1BY. Tapes from the OU's second-level course 'Man's Religious Quest' include Hinduism.

Oxfam, Education Department, 274 Banbury Road, Oxford, OX2 7DZ. Books, slide packs and picture sets; also films for hire. Most concern problems and development in the Third World, but material on Hindu life is included.

Pictorial Charts Educational Trust, 27 Kirchen Road, London W13 0UD. Colourful wallcharts.

Ramakrishna Vedanta Centre, Unity House, Bourne End, Bucks. Distributes a large number of books for young readers, particularly those in the Advaita Ashrama series, suitable for work with primary school children.

Regional Religious Education Centre, Westhill College, Selly Oak, Birmingham, B29 6LL. Produces resource lists, gives advice and runs courses on the teaching of Hinduism.

Religious Education In-Service Training and Resources Centre, West London Institute of Higher Education, Borough Road, Isleworth, Middlesex. Literature, courses and advice.

Resource Centre for Multiracial Education, 165A Cromwell Road, Peterborough, PE1 2EL.

School of Oriental and African Studies, Extramural Division, Malet Street, London WC1E 7HP. Publishes books on the teaching of non-Christian religions, including Hinduism; keeps a stock of resources, and a catalogue of audio-visual material. Visits can be arranged and speakers provided.

Shap Working Party on World Religions in Education, West Sussex Institute of Higher Education, Bishop Otter College, Chichester, Sussex. Organizes conferences and co-ordinates work on world religions in education. An annual *Shap Mailing* and *Calendar of Religious Festivals* are available at modest cost from Peter Woodward, 7 Alderbrook Road, Solihull, West Midlands, B91 1NH.

Victoria and Albert Museum, Cromwell Road, London SW7.

Voluntary Committee on Overseas Aid and Development (VCOAD), Parnell House, 25 Wilton Road, London SW1. Pictures, maps, slides and classroom folders.

DERMOT HASTINGS KILLINGLEY was born in Liverpool in 1935. He was educated at Birkenhead School and Merton College, Oxford. He graduated
with honours in Classical Moderations and Oriental Languages in 1959.
Later, he studied Middle Iranian languages and Indian philosophy at the
School of Oriental and African Studies. In 1978 he was awarded a Ph.D.
for his work on Rammohun Roy's interpretation of the Vedānta. He has
taught Sanskrit and Indian Studies at the University of Malaya. Since
1970 he has taught Sanskrit and Hinduism at the University of Newcastle
where he is Senior Lecturer in Religious Studies. He is interested in
ancient and modern Hinduism and is currently working on a commentary on
the Kaṭha Upaniṣad as well as on a Sanskrit teaching book. He has published articles on the Sanskrit language, Hinduism, and religious education. He has also published *The Only True God: Works on Religion*, a
set of translations from the Bengali and Sanskrit works of Rammohun Roy

SIEW-YUE KILLINGLEY was born in Kuala Lumpur in 1940. She was educated at St. Mary's School, Kuala Lumpur, and at the University of
Malaya, where she took an honours degree in English in 1963 and a
master's degree in linguistics in 1966. Later, she studied phonetics
and linguistics at the School of Oriental and African Studies, and was
awarded a Ph.D. in 1972 for her work on Cantonese grammar. She has
taught in various schools in Malaya as well as at the University of
Malaya. From 1972 until her redundancy in 1980, she taught at St.
Mary's College of Education, Newcastle, where she was Senior Lecturer
in English. She has also taught linguistics and English part-time at
the University of Newcastle—in the School of English, the Further
Professional Studies Division, and the Department of Speech. She has
published articles on aspects of phonetics and linguistics, and four
books on the Chinese language. She has also published stories and
poems, including *The Pottery Ring: A Fairy Tale for the Young and Old*,
(with Percy Lovell) *Song-pageant from Christmas to Easter, with Two
Settings*, and *Where No Poppies Blow: Poems of War and Conflict*.

VIVIEN CLARE NOWICKI was born in Accrington, Lancashire, in 1944. She
was educated at Accrington High School for Girls, Cockermouth Grammar
School and the University of Newcastle upon Tyne. She graduated with
honours in Theology in 1966. She has been Head of Religious Education
at Gosforth Grammar School, Newcastle, and at the Duchess's Grammar
School, Alnwick. From 1971 until her redundancy in 1977, she taught
at Northern Counties College of Education, Newcastle, where she was
Lecturer in Religious Studies. Since 1981 she has taught Religious
Studies part-time at Ponteland High School, Northumberland. She is
interested in aspects of early Christian eschatology and is currently
working on the subject for an M.Litt. degree.

HARI PRASAD MOHANLAL SHUKLA was born in Kampala in 1933 and was educated at Old Kampala Secondary School. In 1962 he was awarded a
Certificate in Education by Exeter University and in 1979 he was
awarded a B.Ed. by the Open University. He taught English in Kenya
from 1957 to 1972. In 1973 he ran the Scunthorpe Multiracial Community
Centre. Since 1974 he has been Community Relations Officer for Tyne
and Wear. He is interested in the social, economic, cultural and

religious problems of all ethnic minorities in Britain and has been an active member of the Tyneside Circle for the Study of Religion.

CLIFFORD DAVID SIMMONDS was born in Chesterfield in 1935. He was educated at Chesterfield Grammar School and Durham University. He took a B.A. in History and Religious Knowledge in 1959 and a Diploma in Education in 1960. He also holds a Certificate in Religious Studies from London University. He has taught at Colston's School, Bristol, and at Sir William Turner's Grammar School, Redcar, where he was Head of Religious Education. Since 1971 he has taught at West Denton High School, Newcastle, where he is Head of Religious Education. Since 1974 he has been a moderator in religious education with the North Regional Examinations Board and he is an active member of the National Executive Committee of the Association for Religious Education. He is interested in religious education in the secondary school and is at present editing *A Handbook on Sikhism: Supplement to the Newcastle Agreed Syllabus* for the Newcastle Education Committee. His publications include *Religious Education: A Modular Approach for Secondary Schools*, *Believers All*, and a sound filmstrip for 'O' level pupils, *The Teaching of Jesus Christ*.

Ābū, Mount 35
Advaita Vedānta 74, 76, 97, 100, 103
Afghanistan 89
Africa 94, 101
ages of the world 72
Agni 17, 55
Āgrā 99
aims 2, 6, 15, 18
Airāvata 57, 58
Akbar 90, 98
Allāhābād 35, 36
Ambā 50, 55
amrita 55
Amshuman 63
animals 8, 15, 16, 24, 54, 72
anjali 27
Arabic 90
āratī 17, 26, 32, 69
Arjuna 67, 80
artha (worldly power) 74
Ārya Samāj 40, 76, 93, 95
Aryan 51, 82, 83, 86, 90
Ashoka 88, 89, 97
āshrama 29
astrology 45, 47
Atharva-Veda 79
ātman 16, 73, 75
Aurangzeb 90, 99
avatār 54, 62, 64, 68, 80

Baladeva 75
Bali 39, 54
Bangladesh 3, 93
bathing 15, 31, 34, 35, 36, 41, 85
Behar 94
Benares: see Vārānasī
Bengal, Bengali 4, 38, 51, 80, 93, 98, 99
Bhagavadgītā 3, 20, 24, 32, 50, 67, 73, 78, 80, 88, 92, 101, 103
Bhāgavata Purāna 37
Bhagīratha 64, 65
bhajan 40
bhakti 44, 48, 62, 67, 73, 75, 81, 88, 90, 98, 99
Bhakti Vedānta Swāmī 77
Bhutan 91, 93
bilva 40
Bombay 91
Brahmā 38, 51, 52, 58, 62, 64, 68
brahmachārī: see student

Brahman 20, 23, 26, 50, 73, 75, 76, 79, 86, 103
Brāhmanas 79
brahmin 11, 24, 29, 47, 48, 73, 81, 83, 86, 87, 88, 89, 95
Brāhmo Samāj 77, 92, 99
Britain, British 21, 33, 34, 40, 45, 46, 47, 76, 82, 83, 90, 91
Buddha 54, 73, 97, 101
Buddhism 48, 72, 81, 82, 83, 88, 97

Calcutta 54, 91
calendar 37
caste 20, 41, 43, 44, 45, 47, 76, 82, 93, 94
Chaitanya 44, 67, 75, 77, 98
Chidambaram 35
Christians 6, 72, 77, 82, 83, 92, 100
clothes 8, 13, 15, 31, 39, 68, 82
conception 27
cow 16
creation 51, 72
cremation 17
culture 6, 7, 15, 82, 83, 90, 97
curd (yoghurt) 17, 37, 40

dance 13, 15, 31, 32
darshan 34, 67, 74
Dasarā 16, 18, 38, 42
Dayānanda Sarasvatī 40, 76
Delhi 89, 91
demon 39, 41, 54, 55, 62, 64, 80
Devakī 64
devotion: see bhakti
dharma 10, 21, 23, 73, 80, 92, 97; see also law-books
Dilīpa 63
Dīwālī, Dīpāvali 17, 18, 39, 42
dog 6, 11
Durgā: see Pārvatī
Durgā Pūjā 38
dvija 29
Dwārakā 35, 98

earth 16, 24
East India Company 38
English language 4, 92, 93, 99
epics 79

family 15, 43, 44, 45, 80, 82, 85, 94
fasting 37, 38, 40
festivals 17, 18, 36
fire 17, 29
food, 8, 13, 15, 17, 24, 27, 29, 31, 37, 40, 46, 48, 82, 95
foot 24, 25, 46, 68
forehead marks 25
funeral 29, 46
Gāndhī 28, 48, 77, 92, 97, 101, 103
Ganesha 16, 50, 58, 59, 70
Ganges 16, 29, 35, 36, 63, 69, 87, 94
Garuda 68
Gāyatrī Mantra 17, 24, 26, 29, 78, 87
gestures 27, 68
ghāt 35, 36
ghee 17, 26, 40
Ghose, Aurobindo 77
Gītā: see Bhagavadgītā
God 73, 75, 76, 79, 90
goddesses 50, 51, 53, 57, 61, 70, 85, 92; *see also* Parvati
gods 47, 50-71
Gokula 35, 64
gopuram 31, 33
Govinda: *see* Krishna
Gujarat 52, 75, 89, 94, 95
guru 47, 67, 77
hand 70
Hanuman 16, 37
Harappā, Harappan civilization 25, 83, 86
Hardwār 29, 35
havan, homa 24, 76
head 25, 39
hermit (vānaprastha) 29
Hindi language 4, 36, 83, 90
Hindu, origin of the word 3
Hinduism, the term 82
Hiranyakashipu 41, 62, 63
history 20, 82-96
Holī 16, 18, 40, 42
Holikā 41
homa: *see* havan
Hong Kong 94
householder (grihastha) 29
iconography 68
image 26, 27, 30, 32, 34, 51, 67, 68, 69, 71, 82, 86, 95, 97, 98

image, installation of 95
incarnation: *see* avatār
India 3, 84, 93
Indra 10, 55, 58
International Society for Krishna Consciousness 77, 98
Īshvara 50
Islam, Muslims 3, 4, 6, 32, 82, 89, 90, 92, 93, 100
Jains 6, 72, 83, 88
Janmāshtamī 37
Jātakas 81
Jesus 77
Jhansī 99
Jumna 35, 36
Kabīr 90
Kālī: *see* Pārvatī
Kali age 72
Kālīya: *see* snake
Kalkī 54
kāma (desire, pleasure) 40, 73
Kamsa 64
Kānchīpuram 30
Kannada language 80
Kapila 63
karman (action) 3, 72, 73
Kārttikeya: *see* Skanda
Kerala 97
king 23, 32, 42, 89, 98
Krishna 16, 18, 32, 35, 37, 40, 50, 54, 64, 65, 66, 67, 68, 75, 80, 88, 95, 98
kshatriya (warrior) 29, 48, 54; *see also* Rājput
Kumbha Melā 16, 36
Kurukshetra 35
Lakshmī 38, 29, 54, 57, 58, 68
Lakshmī Bāī 99
language 4, 80, 82, 83, 85, 86, 87, 89
law-books 29, 79, 80
light 15, 17
linga 26, 31, 34, 40, 68, 69
Lingāyats 75, 80
literature 20, 78-81
lotus position 26
Madhva 75
Madras 91
Madurai 30, 35
Mahābhārata 13, 38, 54, 62, 67, 72, 79, 93

Mahārāshtra 99
Maharishi Mahesh Yogī 77
Mahāshivarātri: *see* Shivarātri
Mandara 56
Man-Lion 54, 62
mantra 17, 26, 78, 86
Manu 46, 80
Marāthās 89, 99
marriage 17, 29, 33, 43, 44, 45, 47, 48
Mathurā 35, 67
Mīrā Bāī 44, 98
miracles 30, 34, 35, 98
Mohinī 58
moksha 73, 74, 76, 79, 92
monk: *see* sannyasī
Mughals 90, 91, 98, 99
music 13, 18
Muslims: *see* Islam
myth 39, 42, 55, 73, 79, 80, 90

Naidu, Sarojinī 103
namaskāra 27
name-giving 28
Nānak 91, 98
Nanda 64
Nandī 16, 58, 70
Navarātri 38
Nehru, Jawaharlāl 97, 104
Nepal 91, 93

Om 26

Panchatantra 13, 81
Pakistan 3, 93, 94
Pāndava 38, 39, 42, 79
Panjab, Panjabi 89, 94, 95
Parashurāma 54
Pārvatī; Durgā; Kālī 38, 50, 55, 58, 61, 70
Patna 97
Persian 4, 90, 92
pilgrimage 16, 32
play 7, 8, 36
pollution; purity 47, 48
Pondicherry 77
practice 23-42
Prahlāda 41, 54, 62
pranāma 27
prāna-pratishthā: *see* image, installation of
prasāda 17, 27, 31
Pratāp 98
Prayāga 35
pregnancy 28

priest 31, 47; *see also* purohita
pūjā 16, 17, 24, 26, 31, 38, 40, 41, 50
Purānas 37, 79, 80
Purī 35
purohita 47, 86, 95

Rādhā 40, 65, 66
Rādhākrishnan 77, 93, 103, 104
rājā: *see* king; states, princely
Rājasthān 98
Rājput 28, 98
Rāma 16, 18, 35, 37, 38, 41, 54, 63, 68, 80, 82, 95
Rāmakrishna 44, 67, 99, 100
Rāmakrishna Mission 77, 95, 100
Rāma-navamī 37, 42
Rāmānuja 75
Rāmāyana 13, 16, 79
Rāmeswaram 35
Rāmmohun Roy 77, 97, 99
Rāvana 18, 38, 41, 54, 80
rebirth 16, 72, 73, 82, 85, 86
respect 2, 4, 15, 20
Rig-Veda 78
rivers 16, 29, 34, 35, 38; *see also* Ganges; Jumna

sacrament: *see* samskāra
sacred thread: thread-ceremony 16, 17, 24, 28, 29, 78, 86, 97
Sagara 63
salvation: *see* moksha
Sāma-Veda 79
samhitā 78
samsāra 72, 73, 80
samskāras 27, 30, 43, 47
sannyāsī 29, 77, 97, 100
Sanskrit 4, 51, 78, 80, 83, 87, 89, 90, 92, 93
Sarasvatī 38, 51, 53, 68
Sarasvati Pūjā 38
Satya Sai Bābā 95
self: *see* ātman
Shaiva Siddhānta 75
Shaivas 25, 51
shālgrām 26
Shankara 50, 74, 97
Shibi 9, 12
Shiva 16, 25, 26, 31, 38, 40, 42, 50, 51, 54, 58, 60, 68, 69, 70, 85, 86, 89, 95
Shivājī 99
Shivarātri 40, 42

shoes 31
shūdra 48
Sikhs 6, 28, 72, 83, 91, 94, 98
Sikkim 91, 93
Sind 89
Sītā 16, 38
Skanda 55, 70
smriti 79
snake 12, 16, 56, 58, 65, 68
Somnāthpur 89
South-east Asia 94
Sri Lanka 3, 16, 91, 93
Srīrangam 35
stages of life 29
states, princely 91, 92
story 7, 13, 37, 38, 39, 40, 78, 80, 101; *see also* myth
student (brahmachārī) 29
Subrahmanya: *see* Skanda
Sūfīs 90
Sumati 63
surname 28
Sūrya 50, 55
Swāminārāyana 75
Swāminārāyan Hindu Mission 95

Tagore, Rabīndranāth 28, 77, 93, 101, 102
Tamil 55, 75, 81, 83, 89, 94
Tanjore 30
tank 31
Tantrism 75
teeth 24
temple 16, 17, 30, 33, 34, 42, 68, 86, 88, 94, 95
Theosophical Society 44
thread-ceremony: *see* sacred thread
Tirupati 35
Tiruvannamalai 30
Transcendental Meditation 77

Turkish 90
twice-born 29, 78, 86

Ucchaishravas 58
understanding 2, 20, 21
Untouchable 48
upanayana: *see* sacred thread
Upanishads 3, 20, 73, 74, 78, 79, 86, 92, 99, 103
Urdu 4, 83, 92

Vaishnavas 25, 51, 98
vaishya 29, 48
Vallabha 75
vānaprastha: *see* hermit
Vārānasī 36
varna 48, 76, 80, 86
Varuna 55
Vasudeva 64
Veda 3, 4, 24, 29, 48, 68, 74, 78, 83, 86
Vedānta 74
Vijayanagar 90
Vishnu 25, 26, 35, 38, 39, 42, 50, 51, 54, 55, 56, 58, 62, 64, 68, 70, 75, 86, 97
Vivekānanda 44, 76, 100, 101, 103
Vrindāvan 35
Vyāsa 62

water 15, 35, 69; *see also* bathing; river
women 21, 27, 29, 30, 31, 38, 46, 95

Yājnavalkya 79
Yajur-Veda 78
Yama 55
Yashodā 64
yoga 43, 73, 74, 80

Teacher's Notes